DISRAELI GEARS

CREAM

Other titles in Schirmer's Classic Rock Albums series

NEVER MIND THE BOLLOCKS, HERE'S THE SEX PISTOLS
THE SEX PISTOLS

by Clinton Heylin

THE RISE AND FALL OF ZIGGY STARDUST AND THE SPIDERS FROM MARS
DAVID BOWIE

by Mark Paytress

LET IT BE/ABBEY ROAD
THE BEATLES

by Peter Doggett

MEATY, BEATY, BIG AND BOUNCY
THE WHO

by John Perry

NEVERMIND
NIRVANA

by Jim Berkenstadt and Charles R. Cross

CLASSIC **ROCK** ALBUMS
Series Editor: Clinton Heylin

DISRAELI GEARS

CREAM

John A. Platt

SCHIRMER BOOKS
An Imprint of Simon & Schuster Macmillan
New York

Prentice Hall International
London   Mexico City   New Delhi   Singapore   Sydney   Toronto

Schirmer Books
An Imprint of Simon & Schuster Macmillan
1633 Broadway
New York, NY 10019

Library of Congress Catalog Card Number: 97–29049

Printed in the United States of America

Printing Number
10 9 8 7 6 5 4 3 2 1

Library of Congress Cataloging-in-Publication Data

Platt, John A.
  Disraeli gears : Cream / John A. Platt
    P. cm. — (Classic rock albums)
  ISBN 0–02–864774–2 (alk. paper)
  1. Cream (Musical group). Disraeli gears. 2. Rock music—History and criticism.
I. Title. II. Series.
ML421.C74P53 1998
782.42166'092'2—DC21   97–29049
                                                                CIP
                                                                MN

CONTENTS

ACKNOWLEDGMENTS

This book could not have been written without the generous help provided by a great many people. I am especially indebted to Pete Brown, who, when told that I was planning to write a book about Cream, concentrating on the *Disraeli Gears* era, said: "Well, it took about four days to record *Disraeli Gears*—no problem, that's 10,000 words per day." I still miss Sunday afternoon tea at Pete's place in north London. Thanks are also due to the following: Jack Bruce, Richard Carlin, Eric Clapton, Ginger Baker, Tom Dowd, Martin Sharp, Bob Whitaker, Ben Palmer, Liz Baker, David Bennett Cohen, Al Kooper, Steve Katz, Danny Kalb, Jake Jacobs, Don Paulsen, Bob Brennan, Bill Levenson, Joey Helgara, Mitch Blank, Neil Skok; Jacaeber Kastor, Barry Gruber, and Brad Kelly of Psychedelic Solution, NYC; Clinton Heylin, Bob Strano, Martin and Jennie Baker, James Karnbach, Bruce Solomon, Larry Yellen, Arnie Goodman, Bob Defrin and Elin Guskind Defrin, Al Romano, and, as always, Pete Frame.

Last, but by no means least, my wife and best friend, Marylou. Her skills as an editor and tea maker are unmatchable

Note: All quotations in the book, unless otherwise stated, are taken from interviews conducted by the author.

PREFACE

There is a story that Ahmet Ertegun, founder of Atlantic Records, has told over the years, that may or may not be apocryphal. One version of it goes like this:

On March 11, 1966, Eric Clapton, then lead guitarist with John Mayall's Bluesbreakers, was sitting in with Wilson Pickett's band at The Scotch of St. James club, in London's fashionable Mayfair district. It was an after-hours affair hosted by Pickett's record company, Atlantic. He was touring England, and his latest single, "634–5789," had just entered the British charts. In the audience that night was Ahmet Ertegun. According to Ertegun, "There were some people jamming on stage. I was sitting with my back to them, so I couldn't see who was playing, but when I heard this blues guitar solo, I turned to Wilson and said: 'That can only be your guitarist. Man, he can sure play the blues.' Wilson says to me: 'My guitar player is having a drink at the bar.' I turned round and saw this beautiful kid with an angelic face playing the guitar like B. B. King and Albert King put together." The guitar player, of course, was Clapton.

What words, if any, were exchanged between Ertegun and Clapton that night were not recorded, but the young, white guitarist made a deep impression on Ertegun, and a few months later, after Cream had formed, Ertegun signed them to Atlantic as their U.S. label. Little more than a year after that night at The Scotch, Clapton, Jack Bruce, and Ginger Baker would be in Atlantic's New York studios recording one of the landmark albums of the '60s, *Disraeli Gears.*

DISRAELI
GEARS

CREAM

INCORPORATING THE BLUES

When *Melody Maker* broke the news on June 11, 1966, that Jack Bruce, Ginger Baker, and Eric Clapton had formed an as-yet-unnamed new band, it was an otherwise typical week on the London club scene. That week, one could have seen any of the following groups around town: The Spencer Davis Group at The Marquee; The Yardbirds at The Starlite, John Mayall and Georgie Fame at The Ram Jam, Alexis Korner at Les Cousins, The Moody Blues at The Bromel, and The Creation at Tiles. Visiting artists included Ravi Shankar at the Singers Club, Ornette Coleman at Ronnie Scott's, and both Patti La Belle and John Lee Hooker at Tiles. And that was just the tip of the iceberg.

In retrospect, that amount of talent in one place at one time seems extraordinary, but in 1966, it was perfectly normal. While good things were expected from Cream (as Baker, Bruce, and Clapton had officially called themselves by the end of the month), they would have to be very, very good to stand out on an already crowded club circuit—since that's where they would primarily be playing. It was where every good band played, and it was where the members of Cream had been playing for years. *What* they would play, at least in part, would be the sum total of their respective musical backgrounds and passions.

For an appreciation of Cream, it is essential to understand where each member came from, both musically and culturally. Although clubs featuring R&B and jazz existed all over England, London, not surprisingly, had the greatest concentration. And as everyone who cared about good music knew, London had the best club scene in the world (and had since the mid-'50s).

Eric Clapton in the Atlantic Studios, New York, April 1967, during the *Disraeli Gears* sessions.
<small>PHOTO BY DON PAULSEN</small>

It's not surprising that of the future members of Cream, Peter "Ginger" Baker was the first to play the London clubs: he is the oldest of the three (born August 19, 1939), and was born close enough to the metropolis to be considered a Londoner.

Baker became a teenager in a London vastly different from the swinging city of the mid-'60s. It was the era of postwar austerity and rationing, and for most people there was an air of comfortable conformity about the place. By contrast, many young people found the atmosphere stifling, but there were few ways to escape it. For a brief period in the mid-'50s, rock and roll provided an outlet, primarily for working-class kids in tough neighborhoods. But British rock and roll, in particular, never amounted to much at the time. In England, its iconoclasm bred a lifestyle that was not to everybody's taste. The real rebellion was happening in a different musical world: jazz.

Jazz has had a strange history in England. Before World War II, there were few fans of American jazz. Most people thought of it as the music played by dance bands, and they really weren't far wrong. By the mid-'50s, fans of the dance bands gravitated toward what came to be called "Trad Jazz." Trad Jazz, for the most part, parallels New Orleans jazz in the U.S.

"Trad," in the U.K., also covered something called revivalist jazz, which refers specifically to those New Orleans musicians who'd migrated to Chicago in the '20s and '30s (Louis Armstrong et al.) and, as revivalist adherents contended, had taken the music to a new level. There were differences in approach between the two—New Orleans jazz prohibited solos and favored banjos over guitars, for example—but, essentially, it was all good-time music for dancing. Although the musicians might have discussed the relative merits of Kid Ory, Eddie Condon, Armstrong, et al., few of the fans cared. Conversely, in London at least, the emerging Art School/Beatnik population *did* care, and Trad Jazz in all its forms became their property. For the first time (in England, at least) a form of music became associated with social issues such as banning the bomb, liberal attitudes toward sex, and the use of drugs.

Clubs and coffee bars began opening to cater to this new generation, mostly in Soho. These supposedly degenerate haunts included The House of Sam Widges, a coffee bar on D'Arblay Street; Cy Laurie's Club in Windmill Street (later known as "the Scene"), a favored spot for the early Who and the location for what were called "all night raves"; and Studio 51 on Great Newport Street. Studio 51 was also known as the "Ken Colyer Club" and was later frequented by The Yardbirds when Clapton was a member.

This was the environment into which Ginger Baker, teenage racing cyclist and jazz fanatic, immersed himself in 1956, at the tender age of 16. As Baker recalls, "I got a toy drum kit for three pounds. One of those little kid's toy drum kits, but it was *a drum kit.* Then I saw an advert in the *Melody Maker:* this New Orleans band wanted a drummer. They were in Leytonstone [in northeast London] and I was in New Eltham [in southeast London], some distance apart. So I went there with this toy drum kit and told them my real kit was busted and being repaired. Which was really, totally insane. But I got the gig." It's a testament to his obvious natural ability that, at this point, Ginger's drumming experience amounted to "banging around on things" and once having sat in with a Trad band playing at a party.

The band that hired Baker was The Storyville Jazz Band. Not a top band but certainly a reputable one that gigged regularly around London and the rest of the country. With a real job lined up, Ginger needed a real kit, which he duly obtained on hire purchase (a layaway plan) after his Mum had paid the £50 deposit. According to Ginger, "They'd got a new trumpet player, Bob Wallis, and Bob was a big friend of Ken Colyer. After I'd been with the band only a short time, Colyer's band went on tour, and we did the next weekend headlining at the Colyer Club. It was great."

At the band's first rehearsal the clarinet player gave Ginger a set of 78s entitled *Hear Me Talking to You,* in which famed drummer Baby Dodds, who had played with King Oliver and Louis Armstrong, discussed and demonstrated his technique. As Ginger says, "It was the best thing that ever happened to me in my life. Completely amazing. So I was doing a Baby Dodds thing. That's what they wanted me to do, and I was thoroughly enjoying doing it."

By 1957 Ginger was appearing on albums. These include a studio recording with Acker Bilk, Bob Wallis, and a sax player who was to reappear frequently in Ginger's life, Dick Heckstall-Smith. The same foursome also recorded a live album at the Colyer Club.

Around this time, Trad Jazz—strictly speaking, just the Dixieland end of it—became not just a national fad but a fully fledged pop craze.

The pop charts started featuring Trad records, and you couldn't turn on the radio without hearing a version of "When the Saints Go Marching In." The craze lasted less than two years, but in the midst of it, in August 1958, Ginger was asked to join Terry Lightfoot's band—a real step up. Lightfoot's was one of the most popular Trad bands in the country.

Unfortunately, the gig lasted less than six months, due to Ginger's infamous fiery temper and refusal to compromise his music. He was already experimenting and, among other innovations, he started to vary the standard Trad four-beats-to-the-bar on the bass drum by playing off the beat, in the manner of Big Sid Catlett, the big-band drummer of the '30s and '40s—which amounted to a cardinal sin in the Trad world. Ginger remembers that "Lightfoot would go crazy . . . so I did it on a gig in London, on New Year's Eve—a big gig. And I got excited and threw in one of these bass drum beats, off the beat, and he turned round and said, 'I told you not to fucking practice with my band,' and I said, 'Okay, you can stick your band up your arse.' And that was me gone. End of gig."

As a pop phenomenon, Trad was all but dead by 1960, and jazz returned to its normal status as a fringe pastime. Dixieland was still played, but for many people—musicians included—it had become associated with forced jollity and warm English beer. Its adherents were, as singer/writer George Melly once pithily put it, "the sort of people who considered seven pints and a loud fart [to be] the insignia of the free spirit." As a force for social change, Trad had quickly passed its expiration date.

But Trad was not the only style of jazz played, or listened to, in England. Modern jazz had a small but growing appeal throughout the '50s, but it was not for everybody. The rhythms were weird, and no one could dance to it. It was serious and intense and so were its adherents. Generally, the modernists looked smarter (tailored Italian suits as opposed to baggy cord trousers and patched tweed jackets—the uniform of the male Trad fan) and saw themselves as an intellectual clique living in a rarified and separate world in which Charlie Parker and Miles Davis were living gods. For some people, however, rigid musical distinctions were irrelevant. Their attitude was, "If it swings it's jazz, and if it's jazz I like it." One of those people was Ginger.

Ginger had always liked modern jazz or at least the '40s swing bands who were its precursors. Over the next three years he made the transition to modern jazz, playing in dance bands and jamming in small clubs like The House of Sam Widges. Along the way, he learned to read music, a task he undertook and completed in less than two weeks. Doing so was made considerably easier after someone explained what the repeat sign meant in musical notation.

In late 1961 Ginger got a regular gig at The Flamingo, on Wardour Street in Soho, as part of the house band that backed visiting musicians. The Flamingo was an extraordinary place. It had opened in the late '50s but had emerged from an earlier club, The Americana, which had opened just after the war, and was probably the first bebop club in London. The Flamingo continued The Americana's penchant for modern jazz and began attracting a black clientele, many of them American servicemen stationed in the U.K. To cater to their tastes the club started to feature records by artists at the soul end of the jazz spectrum, like Ray Charles and King Pleasure. In due course, Georgie Fame (the nearest English equivalent to Charles and Pleasure) became the main attraction at the club, and the "All Nighter at the Flamingo" became a regular gig for Ginger's most famous pre-Cream outfit, The Graham Bond Organisation.

Bond came along shortly after Ginger had moved on from The Flamingo (probably early 1962) to Ronnie Scott's club, which, despite its seediness, was already the most famous jazz club in England—a distinction it still holds.

"Through the Flamingo gig," Ginger recalls, "I got a new gig at Ronnie Scott's, playing with people like Harold McNair. I worked there every night for several months. Every Monday night was jam night, and on one of these nights this fat guy comes in wearing a blue suit, shirt, and a tie, carrying an alto saxophone. He looked like what he was—a Frigidaire salesman. But he walked onto the stage and blew me away. That was Graham Bond."

An even bigger influence on Ginger came as a result of his meeting England's most famous and infamously self-destructive drummer, Phil Seaman. The two became friends, forming a demonic partnership capable of terrorizing audiences and fellow musicians. Seaman introduced Ginger to African tribal drumming, which became an almost immediate influence on his playing and remains an abiding passion to this day.

By 1962, Ginger was playing in a number of groups, several of which featured Dick Heckstall-Smith, whom he'd known since the Trad days. In the early '50s, Dick had attended Cambridge University and, while there, had been voted "top sax player." After that, whatever band he was in got to play at Cambridge's prestigious annual May Ball. In May 1962, Dick and Ginger were part of the Bert Courtley Sextet, so that was the group that got the gig. Courtley bowed out for the evening, and the band was led by Dick.

Apart from the usual drunk debutantes and free-flowing champagne, the evening was notable for the arrival, at a post-ball gig in town, of an unexpected guest musician. Ginger recalls: "All of a sudden there's this scruffy little Scots guy talking to Dick. And he's going, 'I want to sit in man, I want to play.' He was at the Ball cause he was the bass player with a Trad band, the Jim McHarg Scottsville Jazz Band. So I'm definitely against this, but Dick finally says, 'Oh come on,' so I said, 'Okay let's do something really difficult.' So we played a ballad—I can't remember what, but it was one where the chord changed every two beats. Incredibly complex chord structure. So this little guy gets on and doesn't play a wrong note. He knew his chords, and everybody was amazed. So then we played a twelve-bar after that, and he really kicked arse."

The bass player in question was, of course, Jack Bruce, who remembers hearing "this great music coming from a cellar, and I went down to check it out and saw Ginger, who was playing with Dick and some other people. I knew immediately that I had to play with that drummer. I'd never heard drums sound so good. It was an amazing night."

Jack was born May 14, 1943, in Bishopbriggs, Lanarkshire, in Scotland. Over the years he has tended to play down his musical background, but there seems to be little doubt that he was some sort of musical prodigy. Being accepted by the Royal Scottish Academy of Music at the age of sixteen does not happen to everyone, even in Scotland. In 1972, he was asked by *Zigzag* magazine about those days, and his reply, while mildly self-deprecating, actually reveals a lot about his incipient talent and interests: "I studied cello under the leader of the the Scottish National Orchestra, but I didn't stay long at the Academy. . . . I couldn't make it. Put it this way: I liked consecutive fifths and they didn't." The average rock musician knows little of consecutive fifths at fifty, let alone sixteen.

After dropping out at seventeen, Bruce cleaned windows and played in local dance bands before heading off to Italy with a jazz group. After that, he finally made it to London, only to be hired by another band who were off to Italy. On his return to Glasgow, he was hired by the Jim McHarg Scottsville Jazz Band. In fact, he replaced McHarg himself, who had been ousted by the rest of the band in a palace coup. But up until the May Ball of 1962, at least, they were still using McHarg's name.

Ad for Alexis Korner's Blues Inc., 1962, during the period when Jack Bruce and Ginger Baker were in the band.
AUTHOR'S COLLECTION

After the ball was over, Jack disappeared, and it took Dick Heckstall-Smith nearly three weeks to find him again. "I was living," Bruce recalls, "in this tubercular-type pad in Willesden [a rundown neighborhood in northwest London]." Dick's mission was to convince Jack that what Jack really wanted to do was play the blues.

By mid-1962 a new sound was being heard around the London clubs—Chicago-style R&B—largely thanks to the endeavors of one man, Alexis Korner. Korner had been playing the blues for nearly a decade and, just the year before, had formed Britain's first blues band, Blues Incorporated, with his partner, Cyril Davies.

For most of the '50s the blues had been enjoyed only by a small audience. Despite tours by the likes of Big Bill Broonzy and Muddy Waters (usually backed up by local Trad bands), blues was largely viewed as an esoteric offshoot of jazz. For most of the decade, the only real venue for the blues was Korner and Davies's own club, The Blues and Barrelhouse, on Wardour Street in Soho. In 1960 they lost the club, and in the face of stiff resistance to change by the majority of jazz clubs who refused to allow amplified blues, Korner and Davies finally opened a new club in Ealing, west London, in March 1962. It was called, simply, the Ealing Club.

R&B in the U.K. took off at that point, the reasons for which are fairly obvious: there was a new generation of young kids for whom Trad was little more than a musical joke, and modern jazz was a just a little too abstruse. What they wanted was something with the excitement of mid-'50s rock and roll, but with more depth and perhaps more genuine ethnicity. Electric Chicago blues, along with the music of early black rockers with blues roots like Chuck Berry and Bo Diddley, fit the bill. Once again the initial fan base and fashion originators came from the London art schools.

Ironically, even before Korner and Davies opened the Ealing Club, Korner had wanted to expand the musical base of his group, Blues Inc., by adding a horn section to give it a slightly jazzier feel. Davies was never happy with the idea, but went along with it initially and, in April 1962, Dick Heckstall-Smith was added to the lineup.

Shortly after the infamous May Ball, Dick brought Jack into Blues Inc., and a few weeks after that, Ginger joined as well. "Dick took Jack along," Ginger remembers, "and Charlie Watts was playing the drums. Charlie was a friend of Cyril Davies, I think, and he was a big fan of my playing. He heard that I was not doing very well. I was a terrible junkie at the time, I'd been a registered addict for a couple of years, I was using a lot of heroin and cocaine, and I was a pretty messed-up character but playing good. Apparently, I was a pretty unpleasant person."

Charlie Watts was seemingly on the verge of leaving Blues Inc. and insisted that Ginger be his replacement. Ginger recalls: "I went along to a rehearsal and we jammed and it was really far out, beautiful. [It became] a great band, the first time that straight blues players and out and out jazzers got together in the same band."

This lineup of Blues Inc. was truly inspirational. Apart from garnering an ever-growing audience at the Ealing Club and at their central London residency, the Marquee, numerous aspiring musicians performed with them. These included future Rolling Stones Mick Jagger, Keith Richards, and Brian Jones; Paul Jones, later of Manfred Mann; and a host of others, including, just possibly, a youthful Eric Clapton. Clapton certainly went to the club and recalls seeing Jack and Ginger, but no one remembers him sitting in or even talking to the band members.

By the summer of 1962, Jack, Ginger, Graham Bond, and Dick Heckstall-Smith had joined yet another band, the John Burch Octet, with whom they played on their nights off from Blues Inc. (or, in Graham's case, on his nights off from the Don Rendall Band). This was an original and frequently great band, but, for the aforementioned quartet, it was a last, brief go-round with the British jazz scene. Nonetheless, it gave Jack, and to a lesser extent Ginger, their first opportunity to compose for a real band. Just to confuse things even further, Jack, Ginger, and Dick also had their own trio, which never gigged but was the first trio Jack had played in and would be a harbinger of things to come.

In November 1962, Cyril Davies finally quit Blues Inc., having renewed his objections to the horns. His replacement was Graham Bond. Instead of just playing sax, Bond brought along his new toy—the mighty

Hammond organ. It completely altered the sound of the band, and, by and large, Korner banned its use, except for a special spot in the middle of gigs in which Bond was backed by Jack and Ginger—the first stirrings of what became the Graham Bond Organisation. So good did the trio sound that in March 1963 Graham found them a gig.

Ginger remembers it this way: "Okay, great, we got a gig, and off we went to Manchester. We played at The Blade in the Water, and everybody went crazy. So we're driving back down the M1 at eighty, and Graham says, 'That's it, we've made it, we've won the pools. This is the big time.' And I said, 'Hang on a minute—we've got the octet gig on Tuesdays, Alexis the rest of the week, and a few gigs like this every now and again. Let's be cool here.'"

For better or worse, Graham chose not to be cool. Jack says that, "One night, very soon after Manchester, I came to an Alexis gig at The Flamingo and discovered that I had resigned from Blues Inc., because Graham had resigned for Ginger and me. I didn't know he'd done it." Accepting the wisdom of the decision, if not the way Bond had done it, Jack, Ginger, and Graham hit the road. Initially, it was just the three of them until they were joined a few months later by guitarist and future Mahavishnu Orchestra leader John McLaughlin. This interesting and experimental lineup lasted only for about eight weeks. Around September 1963, McLaughlin left and was replaced by the ubiquitous Dick Heckstall-Smith. This lineup became the Graham Bond Organisation. They also became one of the biggest acts on the club circuit.

If nothing else, no other band could boast such talented instrumentalists. They were tagged an R&B group, which was fair enough according to Ginger: "It was a conscious decision by Graham, Jack, and I to decide to go commercial, so we angled ourselves towards rhythm and blues more than just the jazz thing. The people dug it and we dug It, su It was obviously the right move."

By early 1964, R&B had become a commercial force in English popular music. Nineteen sixty-three had been the big year for all things Merseybeat and Liverpudlian, but with the advent of the Rolling Stones, London regained its supremacy, and R&B records—English and American—began entering the charts.

The Organisation may have been big on the club circuit, but for a variety of reasons that was about as successful as they were likely to get.

Ad for the Graham Bond Organisation at London's 100 Club, 1964.
AUTHOR'S COLLECTION

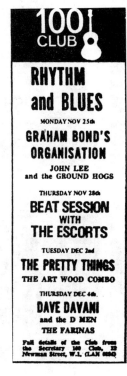

To start with, the music they played may have been commercial in comparison with, say, the Burch Octet, but their modern jazz roots still showed through, and its sheer complexity militated against the possibility of a hit single. They could never compromise *that* much. Jack has a simpler explanation: "We were too funny-looking. You know, just didn't look right. Image is very important, definitely."

Jack does concede, though, that the music was "pretty strange for the time." With the possible exception of their manager, no one seriously entertained the idea that they might have a hit single. Success, for the serious musican, was still based on the clubs and would continue that way for at least three years. If you "made it," you consequently became a pop star and instantaneously lost whatever R&B credibility you may have had.

The chance for the Organisation to play for bigger audiences arose, however, in the shape of various jazz festivals around the country, which, by 1964, were graciously allowing R&B bands onto their bills. The biggest and best, organized by the National Jazz and Blues Federation, was held every August at Richmond in southwest London. Blues Inc., not surprisingly, had been the first R&B band to play there, followed in 1963 by the Rolling Stones. By 1964 there were several English R&B bands on the bill, including the Organisation and a young band teetering on the edge of national success: The Yardbirds, featuring Eric Clapton. By the time of the 1964 Richmond Festival, Clapton had been a Yardbird for somewhat less than a year, having replaced their original guitarist, Tony "Top" Topham.

Not only was the Richmond Festival the occasion of Eric's first actual meeting with Jack and Ginger, but the finale also involved a jam session that included Eric, Jack, and Ginger, as well as Graham Bond, Georgie Fame, and others. "It was obvious even in those days," says Jack, "that [Eric] was an outstanding player."

Handbill for the 1964 Richmond Jazz & Blues Festival, at which The Yardbirds jammed with the (unbilled) Graham Bond Organisation.
Author's collection

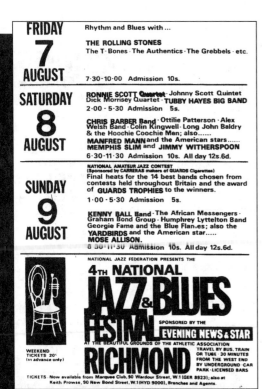

Disraeli Gears/Cream

Now the subject of several biographies, Clapton's early life has been minutely dissected, and the story is sufficiently well known not to warrant great detail here. What is interesting, however, is how Clapton came to be a member of The Yardbirds. Most versions of the story mention Clapton's life at Kingston Art College, where he met future Yardbird Keith Relf, and how Eric was a recognizable figure on the Richmond/Kingston/Twickenham scene. The biographies also detail his growing fascination with the blues; his first band, The Roosters (with future Manfred Mann member Tom McGuinness and future Cream roadie Ben Palmer); and Clapton and McGuinness's ill-fated, brief tenure as part of Casey Jones and the Engineers. The story goes that shortly after Clapton left the Engineers, in October 1963, Keith Relf phoned and invited him to join The Yardbirds. All of which is more or less true. But Clapton's relationship with The Yardbirds goes back much farther than is generally known.

In 1960, future Yardbirds Chris Dreja and "Top" Topham attended the Art School Annex of the Hollyfield Road School, Surbiton, near Kingston in southwest London. The two fourteen-year-olds were becoming interested in R&B, largely through a huge collection of old blues records owned by Topham's father. In time, they both started playing guitar, frequently at school, which brought them to the attention of Eric Clapton, who was two years ahead of them at the same school. Despite declaring that Top's cheap guitar was "total crap," Clapton expressed interest in the record collection and in due course started hanging out at Topham's house. Chris and Top also had another friend, Dave Holt, who lived near Clapton's home in Ripley. Holt, too, was a budding guitar player and would go round to Eric's and learn various licks from him. In turn, he would pass the licks on to Dreja and Topham.

In due course the parties concerned went their separate ways. Clapton went on to Kingston Art School, where he indeed met Keith Relf and, it seems, tried to form a band with him. Chris and Top stayed on at Hollyfield Road for another year. Suitably inspired and despite their young ages, they actually put together a series of ad hoc R&B bands that managed to secure an occasional paying gig. At one of them, they ran into The Metropolis Blues Quartet, who featured, among others, Keith Relf and Paul Samwell-Smith. While dubious about Chris and Top's youth, Samwell-Smith and Relf were impressed by the youngsters' use of amplification (The Metropolis Blues Quartet was essentially acoustic) and suggested amalgamating the best players from both bands, along with Samwell-Smith's old school friend Jim McCarty on drums. The resultant hybrid became The Yardbirds in May 1963.

The lineup remained intact until October 1963, when Top's parents objected to their son turning pro at the age of fifteen and made him leave the band. The vacancy was filled by Clapton. One variant on the story is that Clapton showed up one night and asked to sit in. The band, already concerned about Top and his parents, were blown away by Clapton's ability and duly sacked Topham. Either way, Eric showed up for a rehearsal, and that was that. Chris Dreja later recalled that, "He immediately fitted in. He was obviously so much more talented and advanced as a guitarist, knew more numbers. The whole thing went straight into a new dimension."

The Yardbirds were the quintessential young, energetic R&B group, reaping the success generated by the groundbreaking Rolling Stones. If they lacked the experience, musical ability, and knowledge of a Blues Inc., they made up for it in sheer vitality, enthusiasm, and that prerequisite for commercial success, youth. They genuinely loved the music, however, and their early repertoire was drawn almost exclusively from the "beatier" end of postwar Chicago blues artists—Muddy Waters, Jimmy Reed, and Howlin' Wolf, combined with liberal doses of Chuck Berry and Bo Diddley—very much the standard repertoire of the time. What they added was the "rave up," their term for building a crescendo of block chords. This sound was uniquely exciting to their audiences and gave the band a platform from which to extend and improvise on the numbers—essential in their early days when they played five one-hour sets at the Studio 51 all-nighters. Several writers have suggested that it was only after Clapton joined that The Yardbirds thought of the rave up or were able to do it. But, in fact, it was something that evolved from the very beginning, with Topham.

Like many of their contemporaries, such as The Pretty Things, The Who, and The Kinks, The Yardbirds were able to take advantage of the growing club scene pioneered by Blues Inc. and the Stones. Several of the central London jazz clubs like The Marquee, The Flamingo, The 100, and Studio 51 had already begun

All of The Yardbirds (with the probable exception of Eric Clapton, second from left) thank their press agent for their somewhat limited chart success.

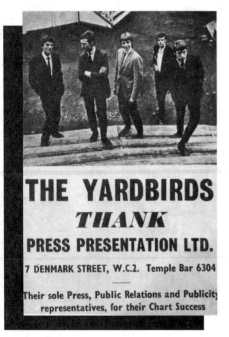

THE YARDBIRDS
THANK
PRESS PRESENTATION LTD.

7 DENMARK STREET, W.C.2. Temple Bar 6304

Their sole Press, Public Relations and Publicity representatives, for their Chart Success

booking R&B bands, as did many former Trad Jazz clubs in the suburbs and the provinces. West and southwest London was the strongest R&B area outside central London; Richmond had The Crawdaddy (home base for the Stones and, subsequently, The Yardbirds); Twickenham had Eel Pie Island, and scattered through-out the area were the various Ricky Tick clubs, the first of which had opened in 1962 in Windsor.

Ad for a Clapton-era Yardbirds gig at one of London's more unusual venues.
AUTHOR'S COLLECTION

Much has been made over the years, not least by Eric himself, of his disillusionment and dissatisfaction with The Yardbirds—as much on a personal level as on a musical one. Initially, though, he was very much part of the band and shared a house in Kew (near Richmond) with Dreja, Keith Relf, and Paul Samwell-Smith. "I shared a room with Eric," Chris Dreja recalls, "and for those six months it was like we were brothers. He was a big influence on the Ivy League look. We used to go to a store in Shaftesbury Avenue [off Piccadilly], called Austins, and he would advise me on what I should wear. I think he used to create fantasies about his life and relationships, and in some way this was reflected in the way he dressed, completely changing his image about every six months. His favorite creature at the time was a chameleon." According to Ben Palmer, Eric actually owned one later on.

More important was Eric's development as a guitar player over the eighteen months he was in the band. If he was good when he joined, he was far, far better when he left. Both Dreja and Yardbirds drummer Jim McCarty recall Eric spending whole days working on one riff, perfecting it and linking it to something else in his repertoire. They also suggest that in the early days he lacked confidence in his playing and rarely took solos. It was only toward the end that he began stepping into the spotlight. They also agree that Eric was something of a comedian. According to McCarty, Eric was "a classic loony. He loved custard pie jokes, and if the joke was on him, he'd stick the pie in his own face."

Eric's ultimate disenchantment with the band is at once under-standable and puzzling. His feeling that they simply were not very good was an honest, if debatable, opinion. That they were moving away from R&B and were getting trapped in commercialism may also be true but misses the point. Much as they loved the blues, they were not dedicated to it to the exclusion of everything else. They were playing music for all of the obvious reasons: it was fun, you could get girls, and if you were lucky you could become famous and make money. And although R&B may have been their first love, it wasn't the only "good" music in the world.

Success at the time meant hit singles, and although other bands were producing R&B-flavored hits, such as The Animals' "House of the Rising Sun" and the Stones' "Little Red Rooster," The Yardbirds never managed to convert their stage sound convincingly onto records. It is not a surprise therefore, that they began to look for some other sound that would get them into the charts. It's to their credit that rather than going for something crassly commercial, they eventually found "For Your Love," which they were able to turn into something genuinely original, and worthwhile but still marketable.

But Eric didn't see it that way. He was genuinely afraid of being sucked into a system that he wanted no part of. How much Eric was simply frightened of success itself is hard to assess, and his attitude toward it has certainly been ambivalent. As future Cream lyricist Pete Brown told Clapton biographer Christopher Sandford: "Eric was scared shitless of fame. . . . On the other hand he loved the goodies that Cream brought. [He had] the need for success vying with contempt for those who bestow it."

By early 1965, Clapton had arguably become the finest blues guitarist in England. A great many other guitarists could perform Chuck Berry riffs, but very few could handle the intricate techniques of the master blues guitarists like B. B. King, Freddie King, or Buddy Guy. It's a curious irony that Clapton left The Yardbirds partly because they were not giving him enough space to express his talent, when, in fact, they were one of the few bands in the country where the guitar played a central role. Most of the R&B bands featured guitars, of course, but generally they were like the Stones, where the guitars were important but rarely used for extended lead breaks. The Yardbirds themselves were fully aware of this, and went out and found Jeff Beck, one of the few people who could carry on where Eric had left off.

It has been assumed that at the point when Clapton joined John Mayall's Bluesbreakers, they were the natural and obvious choice for him. Closer scrutiny suggests otherwise. Firstly, there is Eric's own comment about the Bluesbreakers to writer Steve Turner: "I wasn't that keen on them. I never really thought that John had a lot of control over his voice.

He seemed to know what he wanted to do, but not exactly how to do it. But, I mean, there were very few people around that could do anything properly."

In truth, the Bluesbreakers had neither the sheer musical ability and power of a Graham Bond Organisation nor the rock/pop flair of a band like The Yardbirds. Strictly speaking, they weren't even a purist Chicago-style blues band. Actually, Mayall ran the gamut from the soul-jazz of Ray Charles and James Brown to some rather weak and very non-blues originals like "Crawling Up a Hill" and "On Top of the World," with only a smattering of genuine Chicago-style material. It was a perfectly acceptable mixture, but the Bluesbreakers, despite their name, were even less like home than The Yardbirds for a guitarist craving a strict blues diet.

Despite whatever he actually played, Mayall *was* an authority on the blues, having one of the largest record collections in the country. It is safe to conclude, therefore, that he saw in Eric an opportunity to shift the band toward a stricter Chicago sound with its heavier reliance on guitar. To an extent this is what happened, but during Eric's tenure, at least, the repertoire was never wholly blues. (The classic *Blues Breakers* album contains a Ray Charles number, for example.) Also, during his first spell with the band, Eric was hardly given any more room to solo than he had been with The Yardbirds. If nothing else, this would explain his restlessness and, possibly, his sudden jaunt to Greece in the late summer and autumn of 1965.

On his return from Greece that November, Eric rejoined the Bluesbreakers, at which time they became an incredible band. Whether Eric had simply improved (again) or Mayall let him play more is undocumented.

For a few gigs after Eric's return, Jack Bruce was Mayall's bass player. Bruce was coming to the end of a brief tenure with the group, having replaced the temporarily sacked John McVie. Eric was certainly impressed with Jack's playing, as was Jack with Eric's. Jack told *Zigzag* magazine: "The first gig we did together was this strange club at London Airport—and when Eric started to play . . . phew! I'd never heard anything like it before. We seemed to have an instant rapport, which led to us having long chats about our hopes and aims. I thought that although the blues was great, there was more than that. [The blues] was the beginning rather than the end. But he dug me, and I dug him."

The only recorded evidence of this lineup exists on some lo-fi live tapes from The Flamingo. One track appears on the *Looking Back* compilation, the rest on *Primal Solos.* Despite the muffled sound, they have moments that are extraordinary and support Jack's contention of the rapport, even at that stage, between him and Clapton.[1] The *Looking Back* cut "Stormy Monday" may well be Eric's finest recorded blues performance. His solo is electrifying and is played with an intensity he has never equalled. The tracks on *Primal Solos* don't quite match up; however, the versions of "It Hurts to Be in Love" and "Have You Ever Loved a Woman" come pretty close. The Flamingo performances, taken as a whole, capture this fine band at their peak better than than their excellent, but by comparison, muted, studio album, *Blues Breakers.*

Jack was in the Mayall band because he'd finally been sacked by Graham Bond or, rather, by Ginger. By mid-1965, Jack and Ginger hated each other (most of the time) though they loved each other's playing (some of the time). Both had fiery tempers, and their emotions frequently ran high. As Ginger recalls: "Graham was really responsible for Jack starting to sing and play the harp. The first thing he did was 'Traintime.' But Jack and I began not to get on very well, to put it mildly. He'd blow the beat and turn round and shout at me, 'No, you're wrong!' But I was right, you see. Well a couple of times he got a drumstick on the head for his trouble. He would apologize and everything would be all right for awhile, until one night he'd suddenly do it again."

Ginger claims that on one occasion in the middle of his drum solo Jack turned around and yelled at Ginger that he was playing too loud. Ginger finished the solo and proceeded to attack Jack on stage. Apparently, Jack was only saved by a couple of fast-moving bouncers.

Needless to say, Jack sees it as having more to do with his developing bass style: "I'd switched to bass guitar . . . and I was very aware of James Jameson, the bass player on all those great Tamla/Motown [label] things, and it encouraged me to develop this melodic style of playing, while not going far from the function of the bass—hopefully."

1.　The gig from which the tracks come is dated March 1966 on one of the albums and April 1966 on the other. Jack, however, was only in the Bluesbreakers with Eric in November and December 1965. So unless he sat in for a night—which he denies—the dates on the albums are wrong.

Seemingly, Ginger thought that was wrong and that Jack's bass-playing was too busy. Jack continues: "So I got fired from the band by Ginger, although it wasn't his band. But I refused to be fired, so I used to turn up to the gigs anyway. This went on for a while, and then Ginger made it clear that if I came back, it would be the worse for me. So I decided I should maybe accept defeat. I did some sessions for Marvin Gaye around that time. He was over here, and he loved my playing and asked me to join his band. I didn't, as I was about to get married. But it really encouraged me."

During the first half of 1966, Ginger stuck with The Organisation (who carried on without a bass player, but with a new trumpet player, Mike Falana, and an increasingly unreliable Graham Bond). Jack joined Manfred Mann and would play on "Pretty Flamingo" and arrange the *Instrumental Asylum* EP. Meanwhile, Bluesbreakers fans decided that Clapton was God and that when he took a solo time stood still. All three were feeling the need for a change when Ginger showed up at a Bluesbreakers gig in Oxford and made Eric an offer he couldn't refuse.

STEPPIN' OUT

By March 1966, Eric was again feeling restless and trapped. In public pronouncements he stressed his "loneliness" as a musician and as an individual, in terms that then, as now, make for embarrassing reading. Exactly what he wanted to do beyond a fanciful wish to move to Chicago has never been clear. Privately and occasionally on stage, Clapton was alternately feuding with Mayall and succumbing to boredom. When he speaks about it now, he's more polite about his time with Mayall than he is about his days with The Yardbirds: "I think I could have stayed there [with the Bluesbreakers] forever, I suppose, if I had less of a wandering nature. . . . Up until that point I had been in maybe three or four bands, and so it was nothing for me to stay with a band for six months and then move on. I thought it was a fairly natural thing to do." Eric claims he was not dissatisfied, however, and still thinks of the Bluesbreakers as a great band: "It was the only band in England playing pure blues, the urban blues . . . the gritty stuff. I could have happily stayed there, but there was something about branching out and trying something really new, and it was exciting in a way I didn't know what would happen."

While it is not entirely possible to reconstruct Clapton's ideas during the spring of 1966, a close examination of comments by him and others make a chronology feasible. What seems most likely is that Clapton had a vague idea to form his own band and took a few tentative steps in that direction. In the biography *Eric Clapton: Edge of Darkness,* Christopher Sandford states that Eric certainly asked Spencer Davis Group member Steve Winwood to join a hypothetical band, but that Winwood declined, since he still felt obligated to Davis. Sandford also says that Clapton

18

approached other musicians, including singers, and that they all turned him down, primarily because they didn't think he was serious. Sandford assumes all these attempts at recruiting were for the embryonic Cream. It is more likely, however, that Eric's offers predate any discussions with Ginger or Jack.

The next significant event in this particular chronology was that Ginger, and his then wife Liz, showed up at a Bluesbreakers gig in Oxford in early April 1966. Ginger was about to act on something that had been in his mind for nearly two years. As Liz explains: "I was at the Richmond festival in 1964, when Ginger was with Graham Bond, and Eric was with The Yardbirds, and the two groups had played together. Afterwards Ginger said to me, 'One of these days I'm going to work with Eric Clapton.' He really admired Eric, and it was that gig that put the idea in his head. Anyway, we went to Oxford and arrived toward the end of the first set, and Eric must have been a bit bored because he was playing lying down on the stage!"

Ginger's memory of the evening accords with Liz's, except that he recalls Eric playing while sitting in a chair. "To be quite honest [the music] wasn't happening at all, and the interval came, and I went and saw Eric, and he said, 'You gotta sit in,' which is why I went. So I sat in, and it took off. Eric and I just clicked immediately. It was one of those magic things. Afterwards I said to Eric, 'I'm getting a band together, do you want to do it?'"

According to both Ginger and Liz, Clapton accepted immediately and promptly suggested Jack Bruce as bass player and singer. Given Jack and Ginger's stormy history, Ginger was naturally reluctant, but Liz thinks that Ginger quickly conceded that Jack was the best and agreed to speak to him. It's also been suggested that Eric would only join if Jack was involved, leaving Ginger little option.

Certainly this is Jack's impression. "Ginger came round, in his new Rover, to my wife's mother's flat [where Jack and his wife, Janet Godfrey, were living] in West Hampstead. He had just bought the Rover from the proceeds of writing the B-side ["Waltz for a Pig"] of a Who single ["Substitute"]. He came round and ate humble pie, because what had happened was that Ginger had approached Eric and said, 'How about forming a band?' and Eric said, 'Yeah, but if we do, Jack's got to be the singer.' That's what I heard."

Jack was sick and tired of wearing the white polo-neck sweaters and check trousers required on stage by Manfred Mann, and the financial windfall that he had expected had failed to materialize. Or, as he told *Zigzag* in 1972, "Well, I was still taking the bus and was obviously pissed off playing 'Pretty Flamingo' [Manfred's current hit single]." Under the circumstances, such an offer, even from Ginger, must have been tempting.

If this rough chronology is correct, it seems quite likely that Eric had accepted Ginger's offer before cutting the *Blues Breakers* album with Mayall. Whether Eric's performance on the album was improved or marred by knowing that he was about to leave the band is impossible to gauge. What is certain is that *Blues Breakers* represents the first sustained evidence that Clapton was the finest blues guitarist in England. The album itself is not quite the gem it might have been: the drumming is weak throughout and the addition of horns on several tracks detracts from, rather than enhances, the sound of the band. Nonetheless, it was the nearest thing that England had produced to a real blues album up to that point, and the band's commitment and sense of purpose shine through. More to the point, Eric's playing, particularly on the the slow numbers like "Have You Heard" and "Double Crossing Time," is breathtaking. Of course, a well-recorded live album (had such a thing been possible), would have been better, but *Blues Breakers* is a pretty fair compromise.

Whatever the exact sequence of events surrounding the birth of Cream, Ginger's proposal to form a band must have seemed eminently attractive to Eric, because Ginger's idea was that each member would have an equal say. This democratic approach solved Eric's predicament: he wanted greater musical freedom, but he did not want the responsibility of being a band leader like John Mayall—someone who administered and haggled, hired and fired. No one, it seems, could see Eric in that role, and it was one of the reasons that musicians had been declining his offers.

The members of Cream have rarely spoken directly about those first days, like the decision to go with a trio format or whether Eric had already considered fronting a band. In all likelihood they simply can't remember. Eric came closest when he told his official biographer, Ray Coleman, in regards to Mayall, "I first thought: Well I can do this. . . . God, I should get my own band." He went on to suggest that after Ginger had approached him and Jack had agreed, that he fantasized about "a blues trio! And I would be the slick front man, a white Buddy Guy, the guy with the big suit and baggy trousers—doing straight blues." Certainly it's what Eric's fans were expecting.

Several writers have suggested, however, that Cream was actually conceived as a quartet, with keyboards as the added instrument, and with Graham Bond as the likely candidate. And more recently, Clapton seemed to support this notion, albeit with another musician in mind. "I don't know that I was ever that keen for Graham Bond to join. He was far too jazzy for my taste. I would go after Steve [Winwood] from time to time, but he was pretty embroiled with Traffic." Thus, it seems that despite Clapton's fantasy of a blues trio, the concept of Cream as a quartet was always hovering in the background.

Eric continues: "There were times when [Winwood and I] would speak, and he'd say he was fed up with Traffic, but it never came to fruition. But that's what led to Blind Faith, really: the idea that if Steve had joined Cream, it would have been more of what I had wanted it to be. But I think there would have been a difficulty there, because Jack was the singer."

Jack advanced a more musicological explanation in an interview in *Hit Parader* in early 1968: "We're comfortable with the trio format. If we stop progressing we might think about other members. If we had another guitar, we'd become very limited because Eric plays so much by himself. If we had an organ we'd have harmonic things, which is not our music. Our music is lines and counterpoint. Harmonic changes would limit us incredibly. [But] on records we'll do anything we want." More recently he said: "I can't think of Cream as being anything other than it was—the three guys. At the beginning there was talk of having Steve Winwood in there, but I think it was quite brave to do it with three people, and I'm not sorry that we did."

In terms of whether Cream was actually conceived as a quartet, it's worth considering the session that produced the Elektra compilation album *What's Shakin'*. It was a mixture of unreleased tracks by artists like The Butterfield Blues Band and The Lovin' Spoonful that were laying dormant in the Elektra vaults, along with specially recorded material by Al Kooper and others, including an ad hoc band suggested by Elektra producer Joe Boyd but actually put together by former Manfred Mann vocalist Paul Jones, featuring Jack and Eric on their first official recording together.

While there have never really been any dark secrets about the session, Sandford suggests in *Edge of Darkness* that it took place after Baker, Bruce, and Clapton had decided to form a band but before they went public with the news. Sandford also suggests that Ginger was going to be the drummer for The Powerhouse (the name adopted by the *What's Shakin'* band) but dropped out. The final lineup, apart from Jones, Clapton, and Bruce, included Pete York on drums and, more significantly, Steve Winwood—both from the Spencer Davis Group. The final album is more historically than musically interesting, especially when it comes to the three Powerhouse cuts. The only passable one is "I Want to Know," which is redeemed by Winwood's excellent vocal performance. The other two, "Crossroads" and "Steppin' Out," pale in comparison with later Cream versions, and all three tracks are marred by lackluster production.

While no one has suggested that The Powerhouse was in some way a tryout for a four-piece, or larger, Cream, it is tempting to speculate what would have happened had the sessions gone better—or if Ginger had shown up. What is patently clear is that the trio idea, once Baker, Bruce, and Clapton had settled upon it, was very appealing and presented a strong and focused image. Eric may have initially seen them in the tradition of Chicago-style blues trios, but in the pop world it was unique—at least until Jimi Hendrix formed the Experience. And uniqueness was always an advantage, a superior version of the gimmick beloved of and sought after by pop managers the world over.

In terms of what the new band would play, Eric's vision of the pure blues band (trio or otherwise) was dashed at the very first rehearsal at Ginger's house in June 1966. Eric recalls that "once we were in a room together, it became clear to me that the other two were much more dominating characters than I was, much more aggressive in their wants. So I pulled back and let it take its course into what it first became: a sort of jazz-blues hybrid. . . . I think what really happened was that we found a niche independent of all the ideas that we had individually. It was something that existed when the three of us played together."

As a result, Cream quickly abandoned the idea of being a pure blues outfit. Nonetheless, the blues became, however skewed and altered, the backbone of their repertoire, and several of the numbers unveiled over the first few months became staples throughout their career.

Most of the blues numbers were brought in by Clapton. Some of them were things that he'd played in previous bands, notably "Steppin' Out," which had been a Mayall band favorite, and "Spoonful," which he'd performed, but never recorded, with The Yardbirds. The Yardbirds' version was sometimes as extended as the version Cream played in their last year, but The Yardbirds took it at a considerably faster tempo. Some material was brought in by Jack. "Traintime," loosely based on a Forest City Joe number, had been one of his showcases with The Organisation, as was his version of Buddy Guy's "First Time I Met the Blues," of which no Cream version, official or bootleg, has ever surfaced. It's interesting to note that virtually all of Cream's covers, including "Crossroads" and "Outside Woman Blues," were introduced early on, even if they were only recorded later.

Like the covers, several of the early originals, notably "NSU" and "Sweet Wine," stayed in the live act for most of their career. And, of course, Ginger's drum solo tour de force, "Toad," was still battering audiences into submission right up to the end. The audiences may have expected certain tunes, but the repeated playing of them did nothing to alleviate eventual internal problems. Jack's idea was that material written by him, or the others, would, of course, be added to the live act and/or recorded as and when the songs were ready. But things didn't quite work out that way, since several of the songs Jack wrote for Cream were neither performed nor recorded by them.

Choice of material and musical direction were not the only decisions the new band had to make. At the time, and ever since, Ginger has been ambiguous about whether he viewed Cream as a genuine cooperative or whether it was "his" band, based on the fact that it was his original idea and energy that put it together. He would frequently tell people, "I've got this new band," or "I've put this new band together." To be fair, that attitude can be viewed as a natural reaction and counterbalance to the oft-expressed view that Cream's front man and leader was Eric. That perception has also rightly disturbed Jack over the years, and he doesn't even have Ginger's fallback position of claiming that Cream was his idea. Whoever had the original idea for Cream, it certainly wasn't Jack.

If Ginger had only a third say in the band's music, he more than made up for it with his determination to run the business end of Cream, as he had with the Bond band—a determination that turned out to be both good and bad. On the positive side, it meant that somebody in the band was taking responsibility for getting gigs, negotiating money, finding a manager, etc. On the negative side, his concept of Cream as the natural successor to the Organisation was, simply, maintaining the status quo and ignoring the frontiers that Cream—a new band at the dawn of a new era—might have opened up. As Ginger saw it, they would play the same places as the Bond Organisation (the club circuit), have the same manager (Robert Stigwood), and the same booking agent (Robert Masters)—the sole difference being that Cream would be more successful. This may have shown a lack of vision—if nothing else, Stigwood's appointment proved to be a very bad move—but there were few options at the time for a band like Cream, and Ginger could hustle gigs and money £45 a gig, initially) better than anybody.

Cream made their official debut on July 31, 1966, at the National Jazz and Blues Festival, which, that year, had moved to Windsor. The band went down so well that the *Melody Maker* reviewer claimed that the audience was shouting for them, particularly Eric, to play more, even while they were still performing! The only real problem was that it had been raining steadily for hours by the time Cream came on and the site was a sea of mud. Liz Baker's chief memory of the event is of Ginger slipping off one of the duck-boards leading to the stage and completely covering his brand-new, trendy, white sailor trousers in mud. He was not a happy man. Their relatively short set was comprised of several of the numbers, notably "Spoonful" and the inevitable "Toad," that the band would perform throughout their existence.

Because the hip underground club scene was only just getting started and the university circuit was still in its infancy, the established club circuit, as already noted, was just about the only available showcase for a band like Cream. "There was really nothing else," Jack recalls. "There was the cinema circuit, but that was for more established singles artists. So we were doing what was available." Eric agrees: "We played everywhere [on the circuit] and it meant you could travel out of London without any great inconvenience. And there was a certain type of audience in those clubs that wanted to hear that type of music, and they were educated because they'd been hearing the Stones, John Mayall, Georgie Fame and all kinds of people playing jazz and R&B. The Ricky Tick clubs, especially, had a name for that."

Although, as noted, the university and college circuit was relatively small, the group did play whatever college gigs were available to them. In their early days the most memorable of these took place on October 1, at the London Polytechnic, in Little Tichfield Street, a show that has since passed into rock legend. That night, for the princely sum of two shillings and six pence (i.e., twelve and a half modern pence or about twenty-five cents) one could have seen Jimi Hendrix, newly arrived in England, jam with Cream.

Accounts vary as to how Hendrix came to perform with them that night. But what is not debated is the fact that, before leaving America in September 1966, Hendrix had told his new manager, Chas Chandler, that he wanted to meet Eric Clapton when he got to England. Chas, as an ox Animal, knew Eric and had no trouble making the introduction. It's generally assumed, therefore, that it was Eric who arranged for Jimi to play. Legend also has it that both Jack and Ginger were less than happy about it.

Jack, however, remembers it differently: "I was having a drink in the pub opposite the gig, and Jimi came up to me. He obviously knew we were playing that night. We'd all heard of him through Linda Keith, who was one of Eric's girlfriends. She'd seen Jimi in New York and had told Chas Chandler about him. So anyway, he came up to me and asked if he could sit in, and I said that it was fine by me. I actually took him over the road to the Poly."

Cream roadie Ben Palmer's memory of that night concurs with the standard version, but with an interesting twist: "As far as I remember, Eric was terribly keen on Jimi playing. I think he'd talked it over with Chas. But when he told Jack and Ginger, they weren't terribly happy. No one had ever sat in with them before. But that could just be my assumption. What I do remember is that when I took Jimi onstage and found somewhere for him to plug in, I knew that I wasn't going to plug him into Eric's equipment, even though Eric was the one who'd wanted Jimi to play. I knew that if I had plugged Jimi into the spare channel on Eric's amp, Eric would have pulled it out. Jimi had to go through the second channel on Jack's amp."

Eric's version is a little vague, but his reaction to Jimi, looking back, is interesting: "Jimi came to the show, and I'd heard a little bit about him, but I don't know where I'd heard it. I know that Jimi had heard enough through the grapevine to know that we were the closest thing to what he wanted to see in England. When I saw him I knew immediately that this guy was the real thing. And when he played it was like a rough sketch of what he was going to become. He did all the stuff he later wanted to disown—playing with his teeth and everything. He did it all in the middle of one solo. I'd seen it all done before, mind you. T. Bone Walker and Buddy Guy both did that stuff, and they'd played here [in England]. But this guy was *our* generation, and he wasn't in a suit. . . . I thought, 'If I was black, I would be this guy.' He played a Howlin' Wolf song, 'Killing Floor,' and then we had to carry on the set. It was pretty hard to follow. I don't know whether Jack and Ginger liked it. They said they did, but I could see in Ginger's eyes a certain amount of, shall we say, resentment, as if he thought the guy was trying to steal the show. I think it was just Jimi's way of being."

Memorable gigs like the Polytechnic show were few and far between. For Baker, Bruce, and Clapton, memories of the period have long since merged into a blur of seemingly endless club dates. Nonetheless, Cream was initially a liberating experience and a lot of fun for all concerned. Jack says, "In the very early days we had this car, an Austin Princess . . . and we had something that was very modern in those days, a thing you could put 45s in, like a slot, and it played them, as if by magic. And we had all the latest Tamla-Motown and Stax things and we'd be singing our guts out in the car, and by the time we got to the

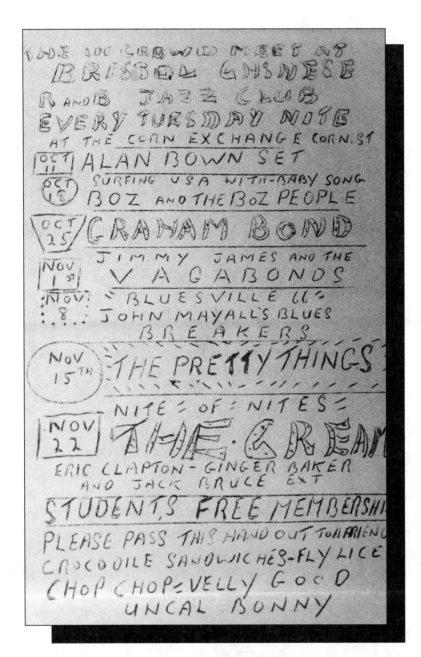

Cream headline on the "nite of nites" at Bristol's Chinese (11) R and B Jazz Club, late 1966.
JACAEBER KASTOR/PSYCHEDELIC SOLUTION

gig, we'd have no voices left. Those are the days I remember with great affection."

Once they had shaken off their initial nerves and a few rough gigs following the Windsor debut, they began fulfilling audience expectations, and, perhaps more to the point, each other's. In several interviews they commented that theirs was the only group that played for each other, not just for the audience.

Even their earliest reviews are enthusiastic and refer frequently to the band's virtuosity: Clapton's searing and dazzling guitar, Baker's thunderous polyrhythmic drumming, and Bruce's driving yet surprisingly melodic bass playing and compelling voice. Above all, it was their collective improvisational abilities that caught people's attention. They had the abilty to stretch numbers to five or ten minutes, without losing focus or dynamics. Only a year later, five minutes was considered somewhat short for a Cream number.

Almost immediately after the Windsor show, the band entered Rayrik Studios in Chalk Farm, north London. The immediate plan was to cut a single. "I think when we started out," Jack recalls, "certainly the big challenge for me, like a lot of other people at the time, was to write singles and to use that form. I mean, two minutes and fifty seconds, to get in everything you wanted to say, to make it musically interesting and also commercial. I think the people that showed the way were The Beatles. We all wanted to emulate that. At least I did."

The first completed tracks were "The Coffee Song" and "Wrapping Paper," in their own ways the two most out-of-left-field recordings the band ever made. "The Coffee Song" was neither a band original nor an old blues; rather it was a straight Tin Pan Alley pop song, with only some tasty Clapton guitar licks and Jack's voice to really recommend it. To be fair, it's quite catchy, but for whatever reason, it was only released, at the time, in mainland Europe. "Wrapping Paper" was a different proposition, and with its recording, or more accurately with its release, came the first real stirrings of discontent within the ranks.

In Ginger's version of events, he had put the band together, and then, "we're like jamming, and Eric's brought in some great things, like 'Cat's Squirrol' and all those blues things, which were just fucking great to play on. We were playing riffs and getting things like 'Wrapping Paper,' and I said: 'We've gotta get somebody to do some words.' So immediately it came to mind that, way back in the '60s, there were some gigs we used to do at the St. Pancras Town Hall called *Jazz and Poetry*. That was 1961, I believe, and one of the poets was Pete Brown."

Ginger was very impressed by Pete, especially with his parody of a contemporary advertising slogan for Wall's sausages. The original slogan was, "Eat well, eat Walls." The parody was "Eat well, eat Walls, shit bricks." The irony is that the parody wasn't Pete's; it was actually the work of Mike Horowitz, his long-time partner in *New Departures*—the correct name of their jazz and poetry events. Upon hearing of Ginger's reminiscence, Pete said, "Maybe I got the Cream gig by mistake."

Ginger recalls that he phoned Pete Brown and said, "'Hey Pete, I've got this band together, and we want somebody to come down and write some words with us.' So Pete came along to the studio, and I introduced him to Jack and Eric, and we started doing a song. I thought we were all doing the song and all contributing. But when the record was released, it said 'Bruce/Brown.' I was astounded."

Leaving aside the question of attribution, Ginger's memory is a little faulty. He and Pete certainly worked together back in 1961, but they had actually met earlier, possibly as early as 1959, at the Café des Artistes in Kensington, when Ginger was playing in one of Dick Heckstall-Smith's bands. In 1962, *New Departures* had a Thursday night residency at the Marquee at the same time that Blues Inc. (with Jack and Ginger) played there on Tuesdays. Because Pete could get in free and loved the band, he saw them almost every week. Throughout the early '60s, Pete was part of the London jazz scene and was particularly close to Dick Heckstall-Smith and, through him, to Graham Bond.

When the Organisation was formed, Pete became such a fan that he attended virtually all of their central and north London gigs. It's fair to say, therefore, that although they were not exactly close friends, Pete and Ginger knew each other through the whole period, frequently attending the same parties. Pete knew Jack in much the same way and is fairly certain that Jack even played upright bass on a couple of Pete's poetry gigs just before Cream formed. Pete also knew Eric, but less well than the others. It wasn't a total shock, then, when Pete heard from Ginger "Yeah, I got the phone call: It wasn't like, 'could you come down and be our lyricist?' It was: 'Could I come down and write the lyric for this particular song.' I remember going down to the studio in Chalk Farm and listening to a playback, and I wrote the lyrics more or less on the spot. That was 'Wrapping Paper.'" Pete's diary reveals that the date was August 3, 1966.

Clearly, Pete found the experience satisfying. "There was something in me that wanted to do this," he said recently. "I had been doing it the other way around, where the words came first and the music was designed to create the right atmosphere. With the jazz and poetry things, there was usually very little rehearsal and very little consideration for what was needed, so it was very hit and miss. But here was a situation where the music was already there and already had an atmosphere and maybe some clear images in it, that I could perceive and could then, as it were, illustrate."

Because the laid-back style of "Wrapping Paper" surprised listeners who were expecting a screaming guitar-led blues, few bothered to investigate the lyrics, which, to say the least, are unusual. "It's about about two people who can only meet in a picture on the wall in an old house by the sea," says Pete. "There was also the image of wrapping paper in the gutter in some sort of out-of-season holiday town. For some reason, I was spending a lot of time in deserted seaside resorts. I also crammed into the song just about every cinema image I had ever thought of, with the result that it's fairly incomprehensible."

It seems odd now, but Pete had no idea he could get an advance for writing the song, or any royalties later on, for that matter. As he says: "One of them suggested that I should go and see Stigwood and ask for money. Remember, at this time I was a pretty well known poet—I'd done the International Poetry thing at The Albert Hall and the whole *New Departures* thing—but I thought I was doing pretty well if I earned twenty quid a week. So I went to see Stigwood and said, 'Look, I've written this song for Cream.' And he said, 'Oh, how much would you like?' Well I thought about it for quite a long time and finally said, 'How about twenty-five quid?' And he immediately whipped out the money and said, 'Here it is.' Vroom. I thought it was incredible."

Jack remembers a day shortly after the recording of "Wrapping Paper" when both Pete and Ginger were at Jack's place in West Hampstead: "Ginger wanted to write a song with Pete, and they were working together, but it wasn't happening. So my wife, Janet, worked with Ginger, and they wrote 'Sweet Wine' together. I then started writing with Pete. So, I got Pete Brown, and Ginger got my wife—kind of. And we've all been living happily ever after."

Pete, it must be said, has no memory of this at all. He readily admits, however, that he has severe memory gaps regarding this period as he was at the apex of his alcohol and amphetamine pill abuse. What he does remember is being at Jack's (without Janet or Ginger), the two of them having agreed to try collaborating. In fact, his diary reveals that it was on

August 4, the day after he'd written "Wrapping Paper." He's fairly certain that the first song they worked on—the title of which they have long forgotten—was something for which Jack had written the first line. It went: "He started off selling fridges to the Eskimos," which may well have been a reference to Graham Bond, who used to sell fridges, albeit not, as far as one knows, to Eskimos. Alternatively, it could be partly autobiographical, as Jack had spent some of his early life in Canada. Pete recalls that "we actually wrote the lyric together, which was unusual for us. Mostly it was Jack's. It was very funny. Too funny really. We were all into the Goon Show, especially the anarchy, satire, and political awareness of it. That was sort of where the idea of the stuffed bear came from. The original plan was to take it on stage with them, but I think it only went to two gigs."

This quasi-Dadaist side of Cream vanished so quickly that the public was largely unaware of it. Pete and Jack's attempts at writing what they thought were pop songs also ended early on. Quite obviously, the two aspects are related. "I had this weird impression of what pop music was, as I had never been involved with it," Pete says. "My poetry had been as obscure, or as communicative, as I wanted it to be, and 'Wrapping Paper' was a mixture of blues and film imagery. Then, for some reason, we got it into our heads—maybe it was just me—that we had to write pop songs in order to be a success. We sat and wrote down all these ideas that were *like* pop songs. But they were one step removed from the reality of pop songs, in the sense that they were really naive but also very hip. How you reconcile those two elements I have no idea."

This period of writing quasi-pop songs produced only five that anyone can remember. "He Started Off Selling Fridges to the Eskimos" (if that was the actual title) was never recorded, and the rest of the lyrics have been forgotten. Then there was "Beauty Queen," which made it as far as a backing track, but again, the lyrics are lost. The third was a quite dreadful track with a long-lost title which was completed and recorded. It contains some wonderfully weird lines like, "You make me feel like a hat stand." Somewhat better was their fourth effort, "Look Now Princess" (of which more later).

Jack and Pete's last pop song was easily the best of the bunch. "The last pop thing we wrote," says Pete, "was 'I Feel Free,' which was a kind of happy accident as far as the lyrics were concerned—although I didn't think that they were quite there. I was obviously very proud that these great musicians were working with stuff I had written, but I was really unsure about what I was doing. After that initial period there was a gap, by which time I was more together and the style changed completely. We started taking on subjects and thinking about what we were writing."

Although it was the Bruce/Brown partnership that would endure, Pete did attempt to write with Ginger, at least up until the time of the release of "Wrapping Paper," in October 1966. Pete says that "Ginger was a great musician. He could read and write music and had some very far out ideas. He was an early world-music person, and he'd written this Polynesian thing that I can still remember the tune of, which he wanted me to write lyrics for. I was living in the centre of town, and he picked me up in his Rover and drove me to Neasden in about ten minutes, through traffic, which frightened the life out of me. [This is not surprising, because it's about a ten-mile journey.] I was still smoking dope and drinking, but by this time, every time I did it I got the horrors. Anyway, I remember being at Ginger's, smoking a joint, getting the horrors and not being able to work very well. But we did get something out that was terrific, but I don't know how it would have fitted in with Cream. We also worked on another thing that had something about gold and silver glittering moonbeams, gold and silver something-or-other hair, which was a love song. It may have been the one that he 'lost,' or the one he lost could have been what became 'Blue Condition'—which I also wrote a set of lyrics for and never used."

In the end the Brown/Baker collaborations came to nothing. Pete feels that he has become, somehow, a living symbol of Ginger's disappointment at receiving no credit on "Wrapping Paper" or, indeed, on any other Bruce/Brown song. If that's true, perhaps the reason Ginger never worked with Pete again is as simple as the fact that Ginger had to continue working with Jack for obvious reasons but was under no obligation to work with Pete.

Jack has a lot to say on the subject of attribution: "It didn't always work out, but I always knew who had written what. Ginger would have been happy if everything had been written by 'The Cream,' but I'm glad I didn't do that. It's not right, and it's not truthful, and it hurts later on." Jack's contention is that he put in a considerable amount of time working on material, the finished results of which he would bring to sessions.

"In fact, I'd written the music for 'Wrapping Paper' two years before Cream. I never forget anything or throw it away. So all of Ginger's thing about how the song just came out in the studio is rubbish. I wrote and arranged 'Wrapping Paper,' and he just played drums on it. As far as I'm concerned, the bass player doesn't get a credit for playing a really melodic bass part, and the drummer doesn't get a writing credit for playing the drum part demanded by the music. With that band, the writing always happened before the sessions." It's hard to fault Jack, especially since he was—and is—a composer in the full sense of the word: he comes into the studio with the completed score written out by hand. He considers that any work done on a song beyond that point is arrangement, not composition.

A tricky situation, but by no means unique. The world is full of drummers who feel cheated over publishing credits. Inevitably, such credits became one of the factors in the animosity that overtook Cream in its last year. And there is little doubt that the lyrics of Ginger's track on *Disraeli Gears*, "Blue Condition," reflect his feelings on the matter. Maybe a compromise would have been to give an arrangement credit to the other members of the band after the Bruce/Brown composition credit. It's likely, though, that such a thing would not have satisfied Ginger and would not have been tolerated by Jack.

So where did Eric stand on all this? The answer, it seems, is as far away as possible. Of the writing situation he now says, "I don't think that I was ever that concerned about the power structure of it. For me, it was always just a question of playing. As long as the political side of it and the success didn't overtake everything, I was happy. We'd go and do a show, and I'd be set free. I know that Ginger wanted everything split three ways, but it's very hard to keep that up. It meant that you had to write under pressure and, as Jack and Pete were very prolific, you'd end up spending more time songwriting than you'd care to. I know that became a bone of contention for Ginger, but I thought, 'Well, I'll just get a Robert Johnson song and dress it up and rearrange it and not really be worried about songwriting.' I was having too good a time playing to be concerned with it."

Eric's comment brings up the question of attribution in the case of Cream's blues covers. To say that the band lacked consistency in this area is something of an understatement. Sometimes they gave sole credit to an individual, as in the cases of Skip James's "I'm So Glad" or Blind Joe Reynolds's "Outside Woman Blues." On other occasions, such as "Four Until Late" they credited a songwriter—Robert Johnson—but Eric took an arrangement credit. On "Cat's Squirrel" they invented a group pseudonym (S. Splurge) for an arrangement credit without mentioning a source, which in this case should have been Dr. Ross. On "Traintime," Jack took a full writing credit, despite the fact that it's obviously based on an earlier number, probably the version by Forest City Joe. And on at least one occasion, "Steppin' Out," Eric obviously tried to come up with a composer, but couldn't decide who it should be. He has released three versions of the tune, with The Powerhouse, John Mayall, and a live one with Cream. They are respectively credited to Memphis Slim, L. C. Frazier, and Jimmy Bracken.

Composer attribution has always been problematic in the blues. From its earliest days performers would borrow from each other, add verses, or change arrangements. Thirty years and ten performers later a song might bear little resemblence to the original. If a performer recorded it, he or she would frequently claim ownership, especially if she or he had never heard the original version. Authenticity and scholarship in the blues were largely unknown until the '50s, when they were imposed by white academics, like Charles Kiel and Paul Oliver. Thus, for the erudite blues musician of the '60s it was a dilemma, because by definition that musician was also part scholar. Should he credit his source, whether it was the correct one or not? And should he claim an arrangement credit or simply maintain, as many had done before, that it was now a "new" song and that he had written it?

Right up to the '50s, writing credits had not mattered that much, since there was relatively little money at stake. All that changed after white rock musicians, like Cream, began recording blues numbers. Skip James was able to pay his medical bills in later years purely because Cream credited him with "I'm So Glad"; Dr. Ross was, presumably, not so lucky.

One might assume that a musician would be justified in claiming an arrangement credit for taking an old solo acoustic number and rearranging it for an electric band with drums, because such rearrangement would genuinely transform it. Clapton would have been doubly justified, perhaps, when it came to "Crossroads," because, apart from arranging it for a band, he actually merged two Robert Johnson numbers, "Crossroad Blues" and "Travelling Riverside Blues," into one new number. Yet Clapton takes no credit, attributing it to Johnson alone.

There may be a simple explanation for Cream's seeming inconsistency in assigning credit: perhaps it depended on how many of the lyrics or how much of the arrangement was changed, or whether a song was in public domain. Even so, Cream's attitude seems very arbitrary.

Whatever the case, in the late summer of 1966, accurate song attribution, whether it was something written by the band or a cover, seemed hardly to be high on the group's list of priorities. What was important, aside from playing live to as many people as possible, was to record their debut album.

In their first five months as a band, during the latter half of 1966, Cream entered the studio whenever they could to lay down tracks for the album that became *Fresh Cream.* They were signed to Reaction, a new independent label owned by their erstwhile manager Robert Stigwood. Press reports from the time indicate that the band signed a five-year deal with the label and received a £50,000 advance. Whether they were forced to sign with Reaction as part of their overall deal with Stigwood is not known, although it does seem likely. Even if signing with Reaction was not obligatory, there was the obvious lure of a record deal and immediate money, rather than having to shop around a demo tape. If they'd held out and signed with a major label, they might not have gotten a better financial deal, but they would probably have had access to a better studio. Initially, they worked at Rayrik studios in Chalk Farm, but by September 1966 they'd moved into marginally better premises in South Moulton Street, Mayfair—a studio called Ryemuse, also known as Mayfair Productions or, sometimes, Spot Productions. It was here that the bulk of the album was cut.

While most people agree that the material is fine and the playing is generally excellent, the record has been universally—and rightly—panned for lousy production. Ginger sees the faults as purely technical: "I believe it was only done on four-track. Now when you're working with such a small track choiceage [sic] and you've got the drums, for example, all mixed onto two tracks, what comes across on the record is what the recording engineer puts down on tape. Now if he's not miked the drum kit correctly, there's nothing you can do to alter that mix. It wasn't exactly a big budget album."

For Eric, the problem was not merely the primitive nature of the studio: "Stigwood was the producer, and neither he nor any of us had any idea how to make a record. We'd run down a tune and play it through a couple of times and say, 'Did you get that?' There was no polish to it, although we may have done a bit of overdubbing. Mayfair [Studio] was only about sixteen foot square, with a control room next door, and no glass to look through. Really though, we were just having fun and weren't taking it seriously at all. And it's unusual for me to admit that, because up till then I'd been extremely serious about the way the music should be. We weren't concerned with making a record, listening to mixes, or anything like that."

Pete Brown blames the lack of production on Stigwood, who had little idea of what the band was about and even less idea how to produce them. Pete distinctly remembers one session when the band had just about reached the end of their tether with Stigwood when Ginger "accidentally" tipped a can of Coke into the mixing console, thus aborting the session. While compiling some of the old Organisation tracks for reissue recently, Pete discovered another example of Stigwood's ineptitude: "They were only working with four-track, and Stigwood filled one whole, precious, track with nothing but handclaps!"

Jack is more philosophical about the recording: "No, I wouldn't say I was happy about it, but neither was Louis Armstrong happy with the way he was recorded with the Hot Five. You have to use the technology that's available, and people loved [*Fresh Cream*]—the primitiveness of it, just as they loved the Hot Five recordings. So we weren't happy, maybe, but that's the way it went down, and we have to live with that now."

Traditionally, really great records have come about as the result of the confluence of three main factors: a state-of-the-art studio; an engineer and producer who love the music and have the imagination and will to stretch the available technology; and an artist with the patience and drive to bring out the best in his or her material. While all three are desirable, any two can still produce excellent results.

While it's certainly true that England lagged behind the States in studio technology—for example, no English studio featured eight-track machines until 1968, and Ryemuse was primitive even by English standards—it *was* possible to make great-sounding records in the U.K. As for producers and engineers, at the top of this tree were George Martin and Geoff Emerick, whose work with the Beatles at EMI's Abbey Road studios is exemplary. Not only did they care about the music, but they were also prepared to push the limits of the technology as far as it would go in order to create the sounds that The Beatles wanted on their records. "Strawberry Fields Forever," recorded in November 1966 (while Cream was making *Fresh Cream*), still stands as one of the most innovative and imaginative pop records of all time.

While Jonathan Timperley, who engineered *Fresh Cream,* and Stigwood were not in the same league as Emerick and Martin, *Fresh Cream,* for all its production faults, was a creditable attempt to transfer the live act onto record. Most of Cream's stand-out material was used, including great versions of blues classics like "I'm So Glad," "Rollin' and Tumblin'," and "Spoonful," along with some of the band's early compositions like "Sleepy Time Time," "Sweet Wine," "NSU," and Ginger's inevitable drum solo, "Toad." By and large, the songs are played as they would have been on stage, with few frills or overdubs, and Cream manages, quite successfully, to capture the spontaneity and excitement of a live performance.

During the *Fresh Cream* sessions, the band did, however, attempt one radical reworking of one of their own songs. At some point, quite possibly the day after the Polytechnic gig with Hendrix, they cut a version of "Sweet Wine" that was never used. Eric's playing on the cut is completely over the top and consists of nothing but feedback. The comparison with Hendrix is obvious. Jack says, "The interesting thing is that Eric was blown away by Jimi, as we all were, but it was a sort of salutory experience for Eric." The tape of this version of "Sweet Wine" is in circulation and much admired by some Cream fans, but in all honesty it's an out-of-tune mess.

As noted, the third ingredient needed to make full use of a studio is the artist's desire to make it happen; as Clapton's comments make clear, Cream were not interested at the time. In fact, all three of the various factors needed to make a really great studio recording did not converge until the following spring, when Cream recorded their second album, *Disraeli*

Gears, in Atlantic studios in New York, with Tom Dowd and Felix Pappalardi at the controls. Apart from anything else, that album was conceived as a cohesive entity, with little or no reference to Cream's stage act.

That the band should wish to make *Fresh Cream* little more than a studio approximation of their live act is not surprising; it's what every club band sought to do, with varying levels of success. A band's album reflected their live act, while, generally, their singles were commercial attempts at cracking the charts. The most ludicrous and extreme example of this approach was, ironically, The Graham Bond Organisation's cover of "Tammy," a real Stigwood special that yielded predictably embarrasing results. Generally speaking, most of the club acts produced albums that, however good they were, sounded far less exciting than their live performances. It's a reasonable supposition that if the technology had been more advanced, most bands would simply have recorded live albums and would hardly have bothered with the studio at all. Unfortunately, such mobile technology did not exist, and most pre-1968 live albums sound dreadful: *The Kinks Live at Kelvin Hall* and the Stones' *Got Live If You Want It,* are two of the worst offenders in this respect.

Curiously, there were some press reports in late 1966 that Cream had recorded a live set at Klook's Kleek, a club in West Hampstead, and that an EP's worth of material would be released from it. It never happened, but a tape from Klook's Kleek, allegedly recorded November 15, is in circulation among collectors. This bootleg tape is the earliest documentation of Cream live. It contains "Steppin' Out," "Sweet Wine," "Meet Me in the Bottom," "NSU," "Hey Lawdy Mama," "Sleepy Time Time," and "Crossroads." It's by no means the whole show, but rather seems to be the second half of the band's first set and, possibly, the first part of the second set. It may be all that was recorded, but it's equally likely that it was the middle tape of three, and the only one that has survived—or at least, that has passed into circulation. At the time, Cream normally adhered to standard U.K. club practice, in that they would do a first set of forty-five minutes, take a break (in which a support band, if there was one, would play), and then do a second set for the same audience. With encores, this second set could run for fifty-five minutes or an hour.

Their performance that night was truly exciting, and if nothing else, shows what an extraordinary rhythm section Jack and Ginger comprised; especially Jack, who, because of the trio format plays what amounts to a hybrid of bass, rhythm, and lead—an astonishing feat. Of the songs on the tape, "Meet Me in the Bottom" is probably the most interesting, if only because it's the sole song on the tape that Cream never released a live or studio version of. It's another old blues of uncertain origin, the oldest known versions being by Amos Easton and Brownie McGhee. It's sung here by Jack, but it's one of the many old blues that Eric has returned to in recent years, since his "rediscovery" of the genre. Of the others on the tape, "Sweet Wine," "Sleepy Time Time," and "NSU" are close in terms of arrangement and performance to the *Fresh Cream* versions and demonstrate what a good job was done in capturing a live performance in the studio."Crossroads" evidently changed little over the lifetime of the band. The arrangement here is close to the one on the *Wheels of Fire* live album, recorded in March 1968. The opposite is true of "Steppin' Out," which, although given a good five-minute workout here, was frequently stretched to three times that length later on, when it included a whole section in which Jack and Ginger would leave Eric alone on stage.

If it's true that the source of the Klook's Kleek tape is an acetate, then the story that it was an official recording becomes more probable. Nonetheless, the quality is predictably poor and may account for why it was never released. The group was undoubtedly wise to stick with the studio, Stigwood and Timperley notwithstanding, for their first album.

Fresh Cream was released in England just four weeks after the Klook's Kleek gig, just in time for Christmas 1966. Despite the production problems, it remains a fine album and an excellent snapshot of the band's developing talents as well as a harbinger of better things to come. Around the time of the album's release, their second single, "I Feel Free," with its ferocious beat, impassioned vocal, and superb—but brief—Clapton solo, had become a respectable hit, peaking at number 11 in the U.K. charts. Its success proved that perhaps it was possible to have a hit without compromising musical principles.

MUSIC IN THE FIFTH DIMENSION

From about 1962—when Blues Inc. began introducing R&B to a wider audience in England—to the end of 1966, there was a general consensus about hip forms of music. Bands may have specialized in one style or another, and fans may have preferred one band or sound to another, but whether it was the country blues of Mississippi John Hurt or the latest Stax soul record, there was an across-the-board appreciation of all music that was both black and American. What caused that to change is a matter of debate, but, for whatever reason, schisms began to appear.

At the risk of applying a little superficial sociology, it was very much a matter of class or, at least, education. In England, working-class (or, less educated) teenagers opted for Motown and modern soul music, while middle-class kids preferred blues, folk, and, in due course, what became known as psychedelia. Of course, these distinctions of taste didn't apply to everybody. Just as Ginger had liked all styles of jazz when he was supposed to like either modern or Trad, but not both, so there continued to be fans who refused to adhere to the new distinctions. But unlike the friendly rivalry between the jazz factions in the '50s, things started to become, on occasion, very nasty by about 1966.

Working-class youth culture in England had always had its violent side. Most towns had gangs that resented anybody who didn't think or look like them. By 1966 their "enemy" was becoming more obvious: artsy middle-class kids were growing their hair, wearing weird clothes, and talking about issues—politics, civil rights, and Eastern religions—

that working-class kids didn't understand, didn't care about, or else disagreed with. As if to emphasize their differences from the artsy kids, the working-class kids began cropping their hair, ironing their jeans, and wearing working-men's boots—unless they were trying to look smart, in which case they wore suits. Violence became an accepted part of their behavior, and proto-hippies, who didn't travel in gangs, became easy targets.

Clubs where all types of music was played, to more or less amiable audiences, became potential battlegrounds. But to suggest that violence resulted purely from differences in musical tastes would be an absurd oversimplification. Nonetheless, life could be tough on the streets, and most kids who didn't belong to a gang developed a keen sense of what areas and clubs to avoid. As time went on, the problem, particularly in London, was that gangs would seek out hippie clubs for the sole purpose of causing trouble.

It should be noted, though, that at the top end of the social scale, at London clubs like The Speakeasy and The Ad Lib—where pop stars including Clapton mingled with film stars, fashion designers, photographers, models, and the like—Motown and Stax records were regularly played and rightly considered to be very sophisticated.

So where did this leave a band like Cream? In this context, Jack Bruce notes: "Even before I started writing things, I wanted to do a Junior Walker song [Walker was a Motown artist], and I remember Eric saying, 'Well that's not right. If we do material that isn't our own, we'll have to be very careful in choosing what we do.' And I gave it some thought and realized that he was completely right"—this, despite the fact that both Jack and Eric loved Motown and soul music.

The exclusion of this material suggests that the band was, indeed, aware of the "right" image for the nascent Cream. And despite the fact that they were pioneers, they too couldn't see beyond the rigid barriers of what they were supposed to play and what they weren't. For better or worse, Motown and soul were thought of, in England, as slick and commercial and at odds with the bluesy bohemian image Cream sought to project. But like most of the musicians on the circuit, they'd each played gigs in tough places where fights had broken out, so any violence based on what Cream looked like or what they played would have been difficult to spot.

Pete Brown does, however, remember an early gig at the Roundhouse where Cream was on a bill that featured Geno Washington, who fronted the most popular soul band in London, the Ram Jam Band. Apparently Cream was all but booed off the stage by Geno's fans, who managed to create a very tense atmosphere and basically ruined the gig for the band and the rest of the audience. Much the same thing happened at South London's Ram Jam club (after which Geno's band was named), a soul stronghold by mid-1966 located in a tough working-class neighborhood.

By early 1967, particularly after "I Feel Free" and the resultant press interviews, it was becoming obvious that Cream was not just another band on the circuit playing the blues. They were playing, or had aspirations to play, music that was much further out. Eric, ever the fashion maven, began dressing like a hippie, with lots of scarves and beads—and his pseudo-Afro hairdo was a dead giveaway. Thus, to a lot of English kids, Cream, along with The Beatles and the Stones, had become, in the local vernacular, "a bunch of pretentious wankers."

The obvious thing, therefore, would have been to allow Cream to play to their strengths, and if nothing else, they should have been booked, as much as possible, into clubs like UFO or Middle Earth—places that made a point of featuring the new psychedelic bands, like Pink Floyd and Soft Machine. Cream may not have been as overtly weird as the Floyd—who started as an R&B band but quickly went into psychedelic overdrive—but they would have received a more than sympathetic reception. At the very least, they should have avoided places like the Ram Jam. But it didn't happen. The most obvious reason is that Stigwood didn't get it. In fact, he never did and, according to Ben Palmer, Cream's roadie, once Stigwood had signed the Bee Gees, who at least sang "real" songs that he could hum, he stayed away from Cream as much as possible.

In the meantime, Stigwood and the band's booking agent, Robert Masters, continued to book them on the old circuit, while at the same time pushing them to be more commercial. Presumably, though, if Ginger had walked into Stigwood's office and demanded that they play at Middle Earth, it would have happened.

It wasn't for lack of contacts on the new underground scene. By then, Pete Brown was fronting a series of bands with names like Giant

Local Sun that were an early fusion of rock, jazz, and poetry, who played regularly at UFO and Middle Earth. Brown and Horowitz's *New Departures* experiments with jazz and poetry are regarded as one of the wellsprings of the underground movement.

Clapton, too, was well aquainted with aspects of the scene. One night at The Speakeasy in early 1967, he was introduced to Martin Sharp, an Australian who was making a name for himself in underground circles as the in-house graphic designer for *Oz,* one of the leading English alternative magazines. *Oz* was infamous for its use of psychedelic graphics and multicolored typefaces, much of this style inspired by Sharp. *Oz*'s founder and editor, Sharp's friend and fellow Austalian Richard Neville, recalled the portentous meeting between Clapton and Sharp in his book *Hippie, Hippie Shake:* "Clapton wore black velvet bell bottoms, a pirate sash and a crushed velvet top appliquéd with velvet suns and moons. It was lot of velvet, even for Clapton. After a brief discussion of Eric Gohill's snakeskin boots, the must-have footwear of the day, Martin brought out a crumpled envelope. 'I've just written a song,' he announced. . . . 'That's great,' replied Eric, another ex-art student, 'I've just written some music.'" Thus was "Tales of Brave Ulysses" born.

At the time, Sharp was living in an interesting old building on the King's Road in Chelsea called the Pheasantry, the former home of Charles II's mistress, Nell Gwynne. Somehow or other the place had become full of would-be aesthetes and people involved with the arts, at least one of whom was related to the queen. Indeed, it may have been through that regal relative that all these characters came to live there. Martin recalls: "I was sharing a studio there with Bob Whittaker, the photographer, but there wasn't enough room for me. It was the wrong design. Through David Litvinoff, who also lived in the building, I discovered that there was another studio on the top floor that was vacant. I moved in, but I needed someone to share it with, so I asked Eric and Charlotte Martin, his girlfriend. Eric was living in a red brick block of flats in some respectable area, so they moved in. I think the rent was fourteen quid a week"—roughly twenty-eight dollars, at the time.

Another, albeit short-term, resident at the Pheasantry was Pete Brown. He remembers: "Eric and I did work on some stuff together, including a version of what became 'Anyone For Tennis,' but nothing was completed. I lived in a tiny room there, and I think the reason they threw me out was because I tried to rehearse my band, the one with John McLaughlin, in my room."

The King's Road, at the time, was an extraordinary neighborhood, a trendy hub of the arts and fashion. But Eric's circle represented a fairly upscale kind of bohemianism, a quasi-underground outpost of The Speakeasy. This was not San Francisco's Haight-Ashbury, with the Pheasantry an equivalent to The Grateful Dead's house. The tenants were far too middle-class for that. If a variety of the Haight-Ashbury alternative culture existed at all in London, it was a few miles northwest of Chelsea, in Notting Hill Gate and Ladbroke Grove.

But as far as Cream's gig list was concerned, the underground—upscale or down—might as well not have existed. The most culturally enlightened places they were playing were occasional colleges or universities, but that circuit was still in its infancy. The band's only real change (and, again, they were following Ginger's Bond Organisation game plan) was playing on the Continent, but the venues there weren't really much different. As Jack recalls: "It was just northern Europe really, in those days. Nobody played in Italy or Spain or places like that. We did a lot of gigs in Scandinavia in town halls and in similar places in Germany. We were very successful, but once again we were quite simply playing in the places that were available to us. There were no big gigs back then for bands like us."

The northern Europeans took to the band very quickly. A possible reason is proposed by Eric: "I know that it has been the same for many American musicians who have found their way over there. Many jazz and blues artists have found tremendous audiences in Scandinavia and France and ended up living there. There is obviously no racial situation for them to deal with, and there's an easy acceptance of that kind of music and great enthusiasm for it."

Success in mainland Europe may have been rewarding, but for most Brits who grew up in the postwar era, the real promised land was the States. As Jack recalls: "We were brought up with American culture. That was as much a part of our background as the Dandy or Beano [English kids' comics] . . . and I think we were always in awe of the music. We were very aware that the only way to progress was to go to the States. We knew that would be the only thing to do, musically, and because we were very much into the blues, it seemed obvious to go to Chicago."

Given the band's musical tastes, Chicago was a natural choice. But it's a measure of how much the American music scene was changing and how much Cream's music was evolving, that San Francisco and New York, once they played there, had a greater impact on them (and vice versa) than Chicago.

Throughout the first three months of 1967, there were rumors in the English music press of an impending American tour for the band. Their American record company was Atlantic (through their subsidiary label, Atco), who released the first U.S. Cream single, "I Feel Free," in January—although they didn't release the group's album until March and, in the process, slightly changed the track listing by substituting "I Feel Free" for "Spoonful." (Whether this change strengthened the album or weakened it is a moot point—they're both good tracks. The Atco release follows the standard American practice of including current or recent singles. In England, singles tended to be excluded from album releases. This industry-wide policy may have been motivated by financial considerations: if the album contained the single, the single's sales would suffer. A more generous view assumes that the buyer had already purchased the single and deserved all-new material.)

At the end of January it was announced that RSO (the Robert Stigwood Organisation) had merged with NEMS, the company run by The Beatles' manager, Brian Epstein—something that, in theory, would add extra clout to negotiations for a U.S. visit. In fact, Epstein was allegedly doing just that in early March, when a slight problem arose. The promo film the band had made for "I Feel Free" had been banned in the States on religious grounds. This seemingly innocuous piece showed the group dressed as monks, cavorting in the Old Deer Park in Richmond, smoking cigarettes, with Ginger wearing an old Brigade of Guards helmet. Of course the whole banned-in-America story could easily have been publicity hype, along the lines of the legendary story about Hendrix being thrown off the Monkees tour later in the year for offending the Daughters of the American Revolution.

One totally preposterous report from this period was the press announcement in February alleging that Cream would be appearing in a major motion picture to be shot the following summer in either Paris or Rome. They would not only sing and play, but act as well!

Finally, on March 11, 1967, it was announced that Cream was scheduled to play in New York at the end of the month. They were booked for nine days, starting March 25, on The Murray the K Show, a multi-act extravaganza, worse in its own way than any of the package shows that Eric had endured with The Yardbirds and that Jack and Ginger had undertaken with The Organisation. But at least it was America.

Murray the K, the self-styled "Fifth Beatle," had been organizing pop package shows for years. In the past he'd been able to guarantee hordes of youngsters showing up to scream and applaud their way through the fifty-odd performances that these week-long spectaculars showcased.

Previously, Murray had booked only teen-oriented pop acts, most of whom were used to, and probably expected, the mind-numbing regimentation of these kinds of shows. But this was 1967, and Murray had sniffed the air and decided that something new was going on, but what it was wasn't exactly clear. That year's Easter show was going to be different; something in tune with the times, with a little bit of that hippie stuff thrown in. The new show, called "Music In the Fifth Dimension," was to take place at the RKO Theater on 58th Street. The poster promised "Total Audience Involvement" and boasted "At Last! It's Here! The First New Presentation of Today's Music!" as well as "Full Dimensional Sight and Sound."

Although not all of the acts were booked to play every single show, the full lineup was Mitch Ryder, Wilson Pickett, Cream, The Who, Jim and Jean (a local NYC folk duo), The Chicago Loop, Mandala (from Canada and featuring future members of The James Gang), The Blues Project, and The Hardly Worthit Players, a comedy troupe. Smokey Robinson was billed, but didn't appear. Nor, as far as one can tell, did Simon and Garfunkel. They were one of the single-performance-only guest artists, who also included Phil Ochs, The Blues Magoos, and The Young Rascals. Lest one should forget, there was also Murray's wife, Jackie, and her dance troupe, The K girls.

So how did Cream, who had virtually no reputation in the States, get onto this stellar bill? Seemingly, Murray desperately wanted Mitch Ryder on the show, but Mitch wasn't interested. Ryder's New York–based agent, the legendary Frank Barsalona, attempted various ways to dissuade

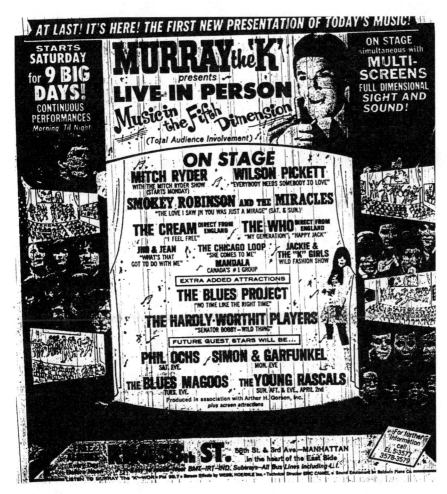

Murray. First, he asked for an absurd amount of money that Murray, unexpectedly, agreed to pay. Pondering his next move, Barsalona remembered that he'd just signed The Who. If Murray had heard of them at all, he surely wouldn't want them. Barsalona told Murray that Mitch would only do it if The Who were brought in as well. Initially, Murray refused, and it looked like Ryder was off the hook, until Murray remembered that The Who were now with NEMS, part of the same deal that brought Cream to the company. Murray was a friend of Epstein's, so he reluctantly agreed to The Who. Barsalona gave up at that point and Mitch, not to mention The Who, were in.

What Barsalona did not know was that when Murray phoned NEMS to negotiate a fee, he was referred to Epstein's new partner, Robert

Stigwood, who handled the bookings. Stigwood repeated Barsalona's ploy, saying, "You can't have The Who unless you take Cream." Murray was not smiling, but the deal was done, and at least he could put "Direct From England" next to two of the names on the poster. It was only after the shows were underway that Barsalona discovered that Cream had anything to do with him. It's also highly unlikely that Cream knew much about these behind-the-scenes machinations in advance.

Cream was late arriving in New York, delayed for two days due to visa problems. The delay gave them a chance to pick up their infamous psychedelically painted equipment from The Fool, the trio of underground artists—friends of Eric's, of course—who went on to work with The Beatles. Long-suffering roadie Ben Palmer recalls that "I collected the guitars and the bass drum skins from The Fool's flat somewhere near Paddington. The paint was still wet when we loaded them on the plane and still tacky the first time they went on stage. The Fool also designed those terrible clothes . . . [which were] hard to take seriously." Indeed. Especially on Jack, who looked even more uncomfortable in his multicolored satin finery than the other two.

Not surprisingly, the shows were a roadie's nightmare. Ben Palmer recalls that "there were five shows a day with the first at 10 A.M. There was a house PA, but we didn't take any sound equipment with us because we had been told everything would be there. But, inevitably, it wasn't. I think for the first shows I hired stuff from Manny's, the music store on 48th Street, but because of the number of acts, the logistics were impossible, and we came to a compromise fairly quickly. We all began using The Who's Marshall amps and speakers—they'd actually brought them over—and we built two platforms for the drum kits which were nailed down and never had to be moved again. We would strike the stage as little as possible."

One of the first locals to encounter the band was Steve Katz, then rhythm guitarist with New York's finest roots-rock band, The Blues Project. He recalls: "They'd asked us to be there at nine o'clock on the first morning, which was, like, three hours before I normally went to sleep. But I got there on time. We knew we were going to be sharing a dressing room with Cream, and I'm sitting there trying to wake up and the door swings open and this lunatic with red hair and these kaleidoscopic eyes comes in, clutching a bottle of vodka—at 9 A.M.—and he looks at me and throws the bottle! He says, 'Here, have a drink.' It was Ginger Baker, and he scared the shit out of me. But we became good friends later."

The whole notion of a band like Cream being on such a show was absurd, as it was for most of the other acts. But Ginger has an interesting perspective: "Stigwood came up with The Murray the K show, which was a classic example of how not to do it. . . . We had become used to playing in the clubs, and our numbers were extended to say the least, and we were supposed to play three numbers in fifteen minutes, every show. Well *one* of our numbers was quite often longer than that. So we played our first set, and what with everybody else overrunning, the whole thing wound up about eighty minutes overtime. The second show wasn't much better."

Jack remembers it somewhat differently, but with the same general horror: "We started off with two songs, then they said, 'Sorry, you'll have to cut it to one.' Then they said, 'That song's too long, you'll have to cut it down a bit.' So it was not all we'd hoped for musically, to say the least."

Al Kooper, in his book *Backstage Passes,* recalls that Cream did, indeed, play three numbers: "I Feel Free" and "Spoonful," choosing sometimes "Traintime" and sometimes "Crossroads" as a closer. Shortly after the event, however, Eric told *Melody Maker* that they had played "I Feel Free" and "I'm So Glad." Whatever they actually played was largely irrelevant because, as Eric also told *Melody Maker,* "the whole thing had nothing to do with the music."

It was equally frustrating for Ben Palmer: "Once Murray had got over the initial shock of The Who destroying their equipment, he insisted that they do it five times a day. I remember the expression on Townshend's face, when Murray told them to do it while causing 'as little damage as possible.' Of course, all the equipment deteriorated quickly. Mitch Ryder and his band performed on an almost life-size castle set that had to be rebuilt for every show. They performed while perched on the battlements and towers, and the whole thing rocked precariously during their numbers. It was never constructed soundly and was in bad shape almost from the first show."

Murray, it seems, took a very direct interest in the performances. Ben says that "Murray held a post mortem after every show, and it was certainly a bad idea to criticize musicians like Townshend and Wilson Pickett, not to mention Cream, without any praise whatsoever. And his

wife kept moaning that she and her dancing girls were not getting enough exposure because of these 'damn bands.'"

According to Eric, "It was a bit like being in a concentration camp." And Jack reckons, "They actually had guards to keep us in." They were allowed out for brief stretches of time, as on Easter Sunday, when members of Cream and The Blues Project headed off to New York's first ever "Be-In," held in Central Park.

Clapton reported to *Melody Maker:* "[There] were 20,000 people just having a good time. There were no stages or admission fees. It was a reaction against materialism." Al Kooper recalled in *Backstage Passes* that he remembered too late that there was a possibility of getting dosed with LSD. He passed on the warning to Jack Bruce and Steve Katz before they'd touched anything, but for Al it meant several unexpected, but fortunately happy, hours exploring his inner cosmos. He wisely sat out the next show.

Generally, the shows were predictably awful, but there were some brief highlights. Jack remembers that "the Wilson Pickett band were amazing, I used to listen to them every night. I'd never heard a soul band in the States before. The point being that although the bands used to play OK in Europe, they never played as well as they did in the States."

The musicians tried to make up for their lack of onstage enthusiasm by jamming in the dressing rooms. Steve Katz remembers Eric playing guitar while Wilson Pickett sang, and ace Blues Project guitarist Danny Kalb remembers playing backstage with Eric. Apparently it turned into something of a duel, and Danny reckons that Ben Palmer declared him the winner. Ben doesn't remember it at all.

The constant interference by Murray, the long days, and the highly regimented atmosphere was bound to take its toll on the musicians. And with The Who's notorious drummer Keith Moon around, mayhem and revenge could only be a short step away. Thanks to a strategic flooding of the shower stall, The Who's dressing room on the top floor was turned into a foot-deep swimming pool. Then a plot was hatched against Murray and Jackie. Jack remembers that "the longest act in the show was Jackie and her dancers, and we all really hated her and thought we should do something really bad to get back at her."

Steve Katz continues: "Cream and us were going to throw eggs and flour at her on stage and stuff like that. The Who, or rather their roadie

Eric and Jack in the sumptuous dressing room, backstage at The Murray the K show.
PHOTO BY DON PAULSEN

Bobby Pridden, was going to put all these explosives all around the audience instead of just inside Keith's drums [the destruction of which was a nightly aspect of The Who's performance]. But Murray got wind of all of this and called a meeting. Somebody went out to Times Square and bought about thirty rubber masks: Frankenstein, Dracula, and that kind of thing. So we have a meeting, with Murray trying to be serious, like: 'What are you guys up to?' And all of us are sitting there with Halloween masks on. It was hilarious. And, of course, Pickett thinks all of these white boys are out of their minds." According to Jack, "Murray told us that if we pulled any stuff like that, nobody would get paid. So we didn't do it, but nobody got paid anyway."

In fact, The Who got paid, but only because their manager, Chris Stamp, went into Murray's office every day to beg for advances. The band was broke due to their usual excesses—destruction of equipment and hotel rooms.

Because no one got paid, it's hard to say what the participants got out of the shows, beyond the obvious hilarity and the excuse to indulge in adolescent mischief and revenge. Dave Marsh, in his book on The Who, *Before I Get Old,* says that "before the ten [actually nine] day run was over, both The Who and Cream were the talk of New York's rock world. Their success with an audience of mainly high school kids confirmed the commercial potential of the British underground acts." Which may be true, although it sounds more like a Stigwood pronouncement—a vindication for sticking his bands, particularly Cream, into this absurd situation. In any case, as Ben Palmer says, "It was pretty demoralizing. At the time, it was a matter of survival, but in retrospect they were quite disappointed. Once it was over there was not much to look back on."

Other things did come out of the show. Eric, in particular, spent many happy nights down in the Village, usually with members of The Blues Project, jamming at clubs like the Cafe Au Go Go. Steve Katz recalls one unfortunate incident with Eric: "It was a Saturday night, and we'd just finished playing The Murray the K show, and Eric, myself, and Al Kooper grabbed a cab down to the Village. We got out on MacDougal Street, which was totally mobbed, as usual. Anyway, Eric left his hand on the post between the cab doors, and I closed the door on his finger, and he started screaming at the top of his lungs. I'm saying to myself: I just broke Eric Clapton's finger. Luckily, by morning it was fine. It wasn't the bone or anything like that, it was just a bruise. But boy, did I feel bad. It's like putting a pen into Picasso's eyeball by accident. Just one of those things you really don't want to do."

Ginger, too, was having interesting nights: "Wilson Pickett's drummer was a certain Buddy Miles, and we used to hang out at this little club on 46th Street [possibly The Scene]. We all used to go down there after the shows for a drink and a jam. It was really a cool time, and I've been friends with Buddy ever since. One night there were two kits down there, and Buddy managed to break a foot pedal on one, and I broke a drum head on the other. They wanted us to pay for them, but I thought we were big stars and we shouldn't have to, so they threw us out."

In the end, the best thing Cream got out of their first visit to the States was the opportunity to record at Atlantic's studios. According to Ben Palmer, "During the Murray the K gig, I phoned Stigwood in London and told him how badly things were going. I'm sure that's when he organized the recording session, because I'm certain it wasn't planned in advance."

As a result, on Monday April 3, 1967, the day after the last Murray the K show, the band entered Atlantic's Manhattan studio on West 60th Street and Broadway for the first time.

BRAIN STEW ON BROADWAY

Before Cream's first Atlantic sessions, the group made some demo recordings at Ryemuse, the studio in Mayfair where they had recorded the bulk of *Fresh Cream*. This tape is now referred to as the *Disraeli Gears* demo tape, and was recorded March 15, 1967—about a week before they flew to the States. Although no date appears on the tape box, Pete Brown's diary entry for that day reads: "Cream demo session. Ryemuse Studio."

The purpose of these sessions is not entirely clear, but there is a good chance that the session was intended to select a new single for the band. The pop world was changing in 1967, with bands at the serious end of the spectrum gradually eschewing singles in favor of albums. Nonetheless, the hit single was still considered a touchstone of success, especially by managers and record companies, who, in the case of Cream, were one and the same. Pressure from Stigwood to produce a follow-up to "I Feel Free" had to be inevitable. And even the most progressive of bands were not averse to the increased stature and material benefits that resulted from a top ten record—as long as it was a piece of music they felt proud of, or at least comfortable with. Neither Jack Bruce nor Pete Brown would have objected if one of their songs had become a smash, especially if it drew favorable comparison with The Beatles, who, as songwriters and single-makers, remained role models for Bruce and Brown.

Equally possible is that the session was also set up to demo material for a projected follow-up to *Fresh Cream*. Jack's memory is that this session had no specific purpose and was simply a taped rehearsal: "We were in the studio to do a demo tape of us going over some new material, and it was all done in the one day."

The reasons why the session took place are largely academic—it's what's on the tape that makes it a vital piece of Cream history. To start with, it's the only known example of Cream at work in the studio. It's not the complete session—certain takes are obviously missing or were not recorded—but the band can be heard running through numbers, suggesting changes to each other, cracking jokes, and putting on silly voices. Despite the obvious seriousness of the endeavor, they seem to be thoroughly enjoying themselves.

More important, of course, is the music. The tape contains early versions of four of the tracks finally released on *Disraeli Gears,* all of which, despite the obvious lack of production values, are intrinsically fascinating, and make for interesting comparisons with the released versions. The first, "Blue Condition," is only present as a backing track, with Ginger humming the vocal line. However, since no one on the tape actually names the track and no actual words are sung, it could have been called something completely different at this stage. The arrangement is fundamentally the same as the final one on *Disraeli Gears,* except that, if anything, it's even slower and more dirge-like. Also, in common with all the other tracks on the demo, there are no overdubs. At the end of the run-through, Jack can be heard to say: "I think that's probably good enough for a demo."

The band made three stabs at "SWLABR," the first two being instrumental tryouts that break down halfway through. Jack and Ginger seem to know their parts, but although Eric knows the changes, he is obviously still working out what to play. Before the second attempt, he tells the others that "I've got an idea," and his playing does sound more confident afterward. The last take (actually "take five," according to the engineer, whose voice can be heard) is complete and has a proper vocal.

This "SWLABR" is quite different from the *Disraeli Gears* version. It's much heavier, far more bluesy, and features Jack on harp as well as on bass. It's also considerably longer than the two-and-a-half-minute album cut: the main part of the song finishes at around three minutes and thirty seconds; they then go into a second instrumental break that lasts for nearly another minute before breaking down. Lyrically it's the same as the album version, except that Jack sings: "Coming looking like you've never ever done one thing wrong," instead of "one wrong thing."

"We're Going Wrong" is a full take with vocals. It's slower and more intense than the *Disraeli Gears* version, although the basic structure and lyrics are virtually the same. It's actually more akin to the live versions the band performed in 1968.

Like "SWLABR," "Take It Back" was rehearsed instrumentally before they attempted a vocal take. On this run-through, Eric sticks to playing chords except for a lead break in the middle; but his playing is assured, and he obviously had a good idea of what he wanted to play on the final version. Ginger's first few bars have a military cadence, which is very effective and fits the style of the song. He seems, however, to have dropped this idea.

While he doesn't actually sing on this take, Jack can be heard screaming and laughing, and this seems to be the very moment that he got the idea for having good-time party noises in the background—the part ably supplied on the released version by a New York groupie chorus. At the end of the take, Jack actually refers to the background voices on Dylan's "Rainy Day Women #12 & 35" and suggests that they should do something similar. On the vocal take, he gets quite carried away with the idea, and between verses shouts: "Do the dog . . . any kind of dog!" The words are fundamentally the same as on the released track, except that it has a different last verse.

Like the demo of "SWLABR," this version of "Take It Back" is also more bluesy and hard-edged than the *Disraeli Gears* version, although the difference is less marked. Nonetheless, it's tempting to speculate what might have happened to their second album if they had not found Atlantic studios, engineer Tom Dowd, and producer Felix Pappalardi. They may have produced a kind of *Fresh Cream* mark two—not in that the production quality would have been poor, but in that they would have attempted to create another studio version of their live sound.

Of even more significance than the tracks that later appeared on *Disraeli Gears* are three of Jack and Pete's songs that Cream never released. "Look Now Princess" is more like a sketch than a fully realized piece. It is taken at a breakneck pace, and although the lyrics are a tad wacky ("Look here now princess, I've got fifteen women called Sue, twenty women called Jen . . . I'm sad") the arrangement is impressive, the time signature is unusual, and it could have been made into something really worthwhile.

"Weird of Hermiston" sounds a bit perfunctory on the tape, but the song works, both lyrically and musically, and deserved further work. Quite clearly, Jack is in control throughout this one. On the instrumental run-through, the bass takes the lead, suggesting that the song is genuinely hard to play or that the other two haven't heard it before, or, possibly, both. Even on the "finished" vocal take, the bass dominates and really drives the band.

Unfortunately, "The Clearout" only exists without vocals but, according to Pete Brown, the lyrics were already written, and a vocal version with the proper words may even have been taped that day; if so, it remains lost. Even without lyrics, the take is quite stirring and features Eric playing some very Who-like power chords. The song builds to a thunderous climax and ends with lots of feedback. Although it's true to say there are no sung lyrics, it's possible to make out Jack and Eric singing nonsense syllables in spoof operatic voices, just below the level of the music.

Jack, of course, finally released versions of "Weird of Hermiston" and "The Clearout" on his first solo album, *Songs for a Tailor*. Also on that album is "Theme for an Imaginary Western," one of the finest Bruce/Brown compositions. It, too, was written by the time the demo tape was recorded and may have even been cut that day, though no trace of it has been found. In fact, the tape, even as it stands, was "lost" for nearly twenty years, during which time Jack and Pete had forgotten about "Look Now Princess." As a result of hearing it again, Jack cut a new version of "Princess" in the late '80s on his *Question of Balance* album.

So why didn't Cream ever go back to the unused Bruce/Brown songs on the demo tape? For Jack the answer is obvious, but evokes painful memories: "The others were full of shit and jealousy. It goes back to the composer-credit thing. I think that was a lot of the reason why they couldn't hear 'Weird of Hermiston,' which could have been a huge hit, because they didn't want to hear. Pete and I were coming up with so many ideas, and they were coming up with one idea a year. It pissed them off. If you're prolific, people can get quite jealous. I couldn't believe it."

Eric, however, told *Melody Maker* in 1967 while discussing possible Cream recordings, "I would like to do a song Jack wrote . . . called 'Weir of Hermistow [sic],' which is a place in Scotland."

Whatever the reasons for abandoning "Princess," "Clearout," "Hermiston," and "Imaginary Western," the fact that they were dropped at all is a great pity: they could have become four of the most innovative and exploratory numbers in Cream's oeuvre.

One caveat that should be added to the story of the demo tape is that Jack dates it as early as October 2, 1966—the day after they played with Jimi Hendrix. Aside from the evidence of his diary, Pete Brown feels that they could not have written all those songs that early. And in any case, he and Jack were still writing their quasi-pop songs at that point.

All but "Princess," he points out, are in the "later" style, begun after his enforced layoff due to his continuing problems with drugs and alcohol. Consequently, he stands by his March 15 date. There is also further corroboration in that his diary entry for the following day reads: "Three more verses required for 'Princess.'" Pete does readily admit, though, that he was in "a very weird state" at the time and that "anything is possible." (It should be noted that, by early 1967, Pete Brown had forsworn alcohol and drugs and he no longer experiences "weird states.") In the last analysis, whenever those songs were recorded, they were indeed rejected, and the tape *did* mysteriously disappear.[1]

In any event, on April 3, 1967, Cream went into the Atlantic studios. From that point on the recording details of *Disraeli Gears* become hazy. The basic problem is that Atlantic no longer has session records relating to *Disraeli Gears,* and none of the band or other interested parties, like engineer Tom Dowd, can recall in sufficient detail what was done.

The original multitrack tape boxes might have contained the information, but in one of the great recording industry tragedies, the Atlantic tape library at Long Branch, New Jersey, was virtually destroyed by fire in the early '70s. The library contained not only all pre-1969 multitracks, but also all outtakes and extraneous and unfinished material. Thus, all that remains for most acts, including Cream, are the mixed-down masters for albums and 45s. In the case of Cream, a few odds and ends were, by accident rather than design, not in the New Jersey warehouse. While undoubtedly of interest, these are confined to unedited versions of released tracks plus a couple of alternate takes. It should be noted,

---

1. At the time of this writing, Polygram Records were preparing a Cream CD box set that will reportedly include most, if not all, of the finished takes from the "lost" tape.

though, that because all of Cream's pre–*Disraeli Gears* recordings were done in London, Atlantic only ever had the finished masters, so any outtakes, etc., for these early sessions were unaffected by the fire.

Fortunately, information can be pieced together from a variety of other sources, which, while not giving the complete picture, adds up to a good guide. First and foremost is the Atlantic/Atco tape log. At the end of every session all multitracks and/or mixed masters of completed tracks that were being considered for release were logged in with the library. Each track was then allocated the next number in a running sequence. A session in this sense may be one day's work or several, one track or a whole album, but as soon as the tapes were finished with and unlikely to be worked on for a while, they were dispatched from the studio to the library. In the case of Atlantic's midtown Manhattan studio in 1967, that simply meant a short walk down the hall. Thus, any date in the studio log is likely to be fairly close to the actual recording date. As will be seen, the bulk of *Disraeli Gears* was cut over only a few days, so the library log-in date can only be out of line by those same number of days.

Therefore, although 100 percent accuracy in dating the sessions is impossible, a reasonable degree of proximity is attainable, especially when taken in conjunction with the testimony of those who were there and with other, ancillary, evidence. More often than not, though, what people think happened is a long way from reality. Stories told by the band and Tom Dowd in good faith over the years are at odds with each other and with the facts, but all contain elements of truth that can be sifted out.

The first myth to debunk is Tom Dowd's "one-session, album-completed-in-three-days" story. As he tells it, "Ahmet Ertegun called me on a Wednesday afternoon and said, 'There is a group coming in tomorrow, and I promised Robert Stigwood that we would record them. Would you try to get the best out of them?' That's all he said to me. The next morning I was in at ten, and at eleven this road crew was delivering double stacks of Marshalls, drums and stuff like that. I thought, my god, what am I doing here? The band arrived, and I was on my own, but we had good communication, and we were recording by two or three in the afternoon. It was very congenial. Felix [Pappalardi] came in either late on the second day or on the third. We worked all of Friday and Saturday, and we came back in on Sunday to clean up and touch up whatever major debacles

Jack firing up Cream's legendary double Marshall stacks. Atlantic Studios, during the *Disraeli Gears* sessions.

Photo by Don Paulsen

there were. At five o'clock, a chauffeur came in looking for three guys. I said, 'They're ready, take them away.' They were driven out to the airport, and they flew back to England."

The Murray the K shows finished on April 2, 1967. For years it was assumed that Tom's story was the literal truth and that the whole album had been recorded in the three-day period following the shows.

More recently, Marc Roberty, in his book *Eric Clapton: The Complete Recording Sessions* (1993), shifts the recording dates forward to May. In his other books on Clapton, published both before and after *The Complete Recording Sessions,* Roberty cites the post–Murray the K dates, i.e., early April. Presumably, he is hedging his bets.

The story is further complicated by the fact that Tom Dowd claims that Ahmet never once put in an appearance during the sessions. Nonetheless, there are extant photographs, taken by Don Paulsen during the *Disraeli Gears* sessions, showing Ahmet and Tom in the studio with the band. They are definitely *Disraeli Gears* photos because Eric still has the Afro haircut—by the time of *Wheels of Fire,* it had grown out. In any case, Paulsen's file dates the session as April 1967, and he remembers that they were recording "Strange Brew" while he was there.

Also anomalous is the fact that when "Hey Lawdy Mama," a track known to have been recorded during the *Disraeli Gears* sessions, was finally released, the production credit was given to Ahmet and Stigwood, with no mention of Dowd, as either engineer or producer. In fact, Dowd has no recollection of the song, and his personal session list does not include it.

Jack Bruce has good reason to remember that Ahmet, at least, was present at the session. According to Jack, Ahmet heard a run-through of "Sunshine of Your Love" and decided that it as well as Jack and Pete Brown's other songs were "psychedelic hogwash." Just to confuse things even further, in a recent interview with Tom Dowd, he suddenly volunteered that he worked on *Disraeli Gears* before going to Europe with the Stax tour—the dates of which coincide with the Murray the K shows—and that, consequently, *Disraeli Gears* was completed in early March.

Proof positive that Ahmet Ertegun and Tom Dowd were both in attendance for at least one of the days of the *Disraeli Gears* sessions. Left to right: Ertegun, Eric Clapton, Felix Pappalardi, Ginger Baker, Dowd.

PHOTO BY DON PAULSEN

So what's going on here? In light of these conflicting stories, the Atco tape logs come in handy for reconstructing the *Disraeli Gears* chronology. They show that on April 4, tapes of two songs, "Hey Lawdy Mama" and "Strange Brew," were delivered to the library. The next library entry for Cream is May 15, when all the remaining *Disraeli Gears* tracks were delivered. This means that to some degree both of Marc Roberty's sets of dates are correct because two sessions took place: one in early April and one in May. Is there any other evidence to support the split session idea?

On April 8, the English pop paper *Disc and Music Echo* reported that Cream "recorded a new single during their recent visit to New York," and that Stigwood had flown out to supervise the session. The following week, they reported that Cream had flown home the previous Friday, April 7, but were going to return to New York in mid-May to finish their new album. The same week, *Melody Maker* reported much the same thing but were more specific, stating that the band would leave England on May 8 for New York and fly back on May 19, direct to Germany, where they would appear the next day. *Melody Maker* also mentions "Strange Brew" as the title of the new single. Neither paper refers to the second visit again, but taken in conjunction with the tape logs, it seems fairly conclusive that two sets of sessions took place.

So how does this tie in with the other anomalies? Tom's memory that the band recorded in early March is simply not workable. The band arrived in New York for the first time the night before their first Murray the K gig, on March 24. The first session was definitely held on April 3, but exactly who was in attendance is in dispute.

Presumably, the original idea was that Ahmet and Stigwood would produce the band, possibly with Arif Mardin engineering. Ginger has alluded to Mardin's presence at the first session, so it's possible. This team cut "Hey Lawdy Mama," but that's all—probably because the band was fed up with Stigwood, and Ertegun wasn't getting on with Jack. It's likely that this was the reason that Ahmet asked Felix Pappalardi to produce.

There is, however, a problem: Tom claims that he engineered "Strange Brew," which was done on April 4, but has no memory of "Hey Lawdy Mama." This leaves two possibilities: either he did engineer "Hey Lawdy Mama" and he's simply forgotten it, or he only came in on April 4, when the group cut "Strange Brew." Equally plausible, but likewise difficult to prove, is that Pappalardi produced only the May sessions. He was obviously around for the April sessions, but whether he actually sat in the producer's chair for "Strange Brew," on April 4, is impossible to ascertain. He did, of course, receive credit for it—along with all the other tracks on *Disraeli Gears.* Another minor imponderable is whether Stigwood attended both sessions in April, although the fact that he is not in any of Don Paulsen's photographs taken on April 4 suggests he wasn't.

Given the known facts and sifting the evidence, the sessions probably went as follows: on April 3, Ahmet Ertegun and Robert Stigwood produce both versions of "Hey Lawdy Mama" with either Tom Dowd or Arif Mardin engineering, and with Felix Pappalardi in attendance part of the time. On April 4, Felix produces "Strange Brew," with Tom Dowd engineering and Ahmet Ertegun around as uncredited consultant. By contrast the mid-May sessions are much simpler, with Felix producing and Tom Dowd engineering.

Assuming that the split-session theory is correct, one possible scenario is that April 3 and 4 were booked expressly to record a new single, and the band was so pleased with the result that they resolved to return as quickly as possible to complete an album's worth of material. This certainly fits the facts—they did complete a single and they did return to do the album—but it's rather too neat. Just as likely is Ben Palmer's previously mentioned statement that there were no plans at all for them to record at Atlantic following the Murray the K shows, and the sessions were arranged simply to appease the band after the ordeal of those shows.

Whatever the truth may be, Cream was obviously pleased to be working, at last, in a decent studio. How much they knew up front about the studio's technical facilities is hard to say, but they were certainly aware of all the great records that had been produced there. In fact, the Atlantic studios at 1841 Broadway, despite being nearly ten years old in 1967, were still rightly regarded as state of the art. Their main claim to fame was that they were the first commercial studios to incorporate eight-track equipment, which, if nothing else, was unknown in England until 1968. Both the studio and its equipment had been the brainchild of Atlantic engineer/producer Tom Dowd.

In 1957, listening to the innovative recordings of guitarist Les Paul, Dowd figured out that Paul could only be producing his unique-sounding records by using an eight-track machine. He then persuaded Ahmet that such a machine would give Atlantic far greater flexibility: they would be able to remix, edit, and overdub in ways that were impossible before. Dowd then tracked down the company that built Les Paul's machine and ordered one for Atlantic. The only problem was that no one made a console that could accommodate it, so Dowd had to design one himself. He worked out what parts he would need, ordered those, and then built it from scratch. For a brief time the equipment was used in Atlantic's original studios at 234 West 56th Street, but it was soon apparent that those premises were too small, and so Tom supervised the construction of the new studio, four blocks uptown.

Tom Dowd is an extraordinary person with a remarkable history. Born in 1925 in New York, he graduated high school at age sixteen and, despite musical leanings, seemed happily destined for a career as a physicist. He was clearly a brilliant student—in 1942 he was asked to join what became the Manhattan Project, based at Columbia University, where he worked on the design of the atomic bomb.

After the war, Dowd traveled for a year and on his return felt the need for a change. He answered a newspaper ad for a recording engineer and discovered that a recording studio was where he really belonged. Not long after Atlantic's formation in 1947, Dowd started doing odd sessions for them. Impressed by Atlantic's approach, both to the music and to their recording methods, he began working with them more and more. By the mid-'50s he was part of Atlantic's legendary team that included Ahmet Ertegun, his brother Nesuhi (who handled the jazz artists), Jerry Wexler, and Arif Mardin. All were able producers and engineers, but it was Dowd who was the real technical innovator. Also around was Herb Abramson, Ahmet's original partner. He was drafted into the army in 1953 (Wexler was supposedly his short-term replacement) and, on his return in 1955, he discovered that the company was doing fine without him. Partly to placate him, he was given his own company, Atco, a wholly owned subsidiary of Atlantic. Atco carried on, but Abramson was never comfortable with the sideways move and left the label two years later. For reasons that are not entirely clear, Cream were signed to the Atco subsidiary; Atco released their records, alongside a curious mixture of artists that by 1967 included Sonny and Cher, Buffalo Springfield, Acker Bilk (an English Trad-turned-MOR musician), Nino Tempo and April Stevens, Ben E. King, and Arthur Conley.

Throughout the '50s and early '60s, Atlantic released hundreds of classic R&B and R&B–related records, many of which were Dowd productions, although he was usually only credited as engineer. His releases included records by Ruth Brown, The Coasters, The Drifters, The Modern Jazz Quartet, and scores of others. With black music evolving from R&B

into soul, the label also moved in that direction, and by the mid-'60s Dowd was intimately involved with the Memphis-based Stax label, who had signed a licensing deal with Atlantic.

Assuming again that the two-session theory is correct, those first two days in early April were tough ones for Jack. He recalls that "it was a very difficult time for me. I was bringing, I think, the best material that I'd written with Pete, and was very, very keen to have it recorded. But when we played it to the powers that be, they didn't like it. They said it's not happening. I'm talking about 'Sunshine of Your Love' and stuff like that. Anyway, [they said] 'Eric's the front man and the singer, so you go over and sit down in the corner and play the bass.'"

Jack now believes he was going through "some kind of crisis, because everything I'd worked for and believed in, I was told was shit. So I had to try and deal with that. I just sort of waited around. And when there was no other material, they said, 'Well OK, we'll have to do your stuff.' And I think what saved it was that Booker T. Jones [of Booker T and the MGs] came in and said that he loved 'Sunshine of Your Love.'" As we have seen, though, "Sunshine" and Jack's other songs would not actually be recorded until May.

So what was Ahmet's problem? One can only assume that he thought he'd signed a straight-ahead white blues band, led by the golden boy from the Bluesbreakers, whom he'd seen a year before: Eric Clapton. Demonstrably, that's not what he got. It's purely conjecture, but, when it became obvious that they would have to "resort" to Jack's songs, Ertegun probably backed off. He needed, of course, to protect his investment, and because he neither wanted to, nor could he work with, this "other" kind of band, he needed someone else to do it for him—someone who understood what Cream was about. With the timely arrival of Felix Pappalardi, he saw a way out.

Felix Pappalardi was another fascinating character with a colorful past. He was born in the Bronx in 1939, attended the prestigious New York High School of Music and Art, and later attended the University of Michigan Conservatory for Music, where he studied orchestration and conducting. That was followed by a stint as a military policeman and as an encyclopedia salesman! Around 1962, he started hanging out in Greenwich Village.

In 1971 he told *Hit Parader:* "I saw immediately that the Village was just alive with new things. Things that either I hadn't heard before or that rekindled my interest in things that I had [heard before]. . . . I was a member of the University of Michigan Folklore Society, where I'd met and played with John Lee Hooker, Howlin' Wolf—all of those people. So I did have a background in blues and folk, which I brought with me."

Also in 1971, Felix spoke to *Zigzag* about his early days: "To begin with, I was playing guitar and singing, then I played a six-string Mexican bass called a guitarron, behind people like Tom Rush and Tom Paxton. I teamed up with John Sebastian and various other people, and we became studio musicians for Elektra and Vanguard as well as accompanying people like Fred Neil in the clubs. It was a great period of time for me, I loved it."

Other musicians that Felix worked with around this time (1963–1966), both live and in the studio, included Tim Hardin, Richie Havens, and Richard and Mimi Fariña, but by mid-1966, his real passion was for a nameless Middle Eastern group who worked at the Feenjon Cafe in the Village. Felix joined the band, most of whom were actually from the Middle East. The one exception was Steve Knight, who later played with Felix in Mountain. They eventually adopted a name, The Devil's Anvil, and cut a highly exotic, and very rare, album for Columbia called *Hard Rock from the Middle East.*

In late 1966, Felix got his big break when he was asked to produce the first album by The Youngbloods, one of the hottest new bands on the Village scene. The Youngbloods' deal with RCA was unique at the time: they were allowed their choice of producer and unlimited studio time. Felix made full use of it. If nothing else he was in a position, as producer, to make sure that his arrangements were recorded properly. In his folk days he'd done hundreds of arrangements for artists, only to have producers screw them up.

The Youngbloods' album was a fairly simple production. Felix didn't really get going as producer until he worked on Hamilton Camp's *Here's to You* album in early 1967. Felix told *Crawdaddy* in 1968: "I had two weeks to do a whole album, and I found myself, like, putting down basic tracks with studio musicians, and then putting Hamilton on, and then putting [myself] on in one form or another: strings, brass, depending on what I heard. And I always knew that that was what I wanted to do."

Around this time Felix started hanging around the Atlantic offices and studio, largely because he thought that Atlantic would be the most sympathetic to his production approach. However, it's worth noting a comment by guitarist and songwriter Jake Jacobs, sometime member of The Fugs, Bunky and Jake, and Jake and the Family Jewels. Jacobs was a Village habitué and a friend of Felix's. According to Jake: "I remember running into Felix on the street one day in early '67, and he started raving about this new English group, Cream. I think he'd just got their first album on import. Anyway he said to me, 'I'm going to produce this band.' And this was before they'd played here."

Felix related one version of his meeting with Cream in the *Hit Parader* piece, and while interesting, it doesn't quite jibe with the facts: "I had sort of taken Phil Spector's place at Atlantic, as Ahmet Ertegun's protégé. I'd gone over there, and Ahmet and I really hit it off. I really loved him. I was in Ahmet's office one afternoon, and Tommy Dowd and Arif Mardin came in and said there were three boys from London and—I don't remember the exact thing, but either [Mardin and Dowd] didn't have time or it wasn't going anywhere, but would I go into the studio and attempt to take over. That was the first day [Cream] was in the studio. In the next five days we completed *Disraeli Gears.*"

In an interview in *Circus,* also in 1971, Felix remembered it slightly differently: "I'd been hanging out at Atlantic for a while. . . . One day I walked in on them [Cream], just like that. I had heard Cream from their first album. It happens so rarely, you know, that immediate spark between people, but it was there with us. We sat and talked and played for hours. I don't remember anything actually being said, but suddenly we all knew that I would produce them." Somewhere in there are, presumably, some grains of truth.

So what actually happened on Cream's first day at Atlantic? Ginger recalls that "We went into the studio without much of an idea of what we were going to do. Ahmet said, 'Play a number.' So we did one of Eric's old blues numbers, 'Hey Lawdy Mama.'"

"Hey Lawdy Mama" had been in Cream's repertoire for a while, the earliest known versions coming from the Klook's Kleek tape (assuming its November 15, 1966, date is correct) and a BBC radio broadcast recorded December 9, 1966. Eric seems to have adapted it from Junior Wells's version, which appeared on Wells's 1966 Delmark album *Hoodoo Man Blues,* with Buddy Guy on guitar. It's also very likely that Clapton had seen Wells and Guy perform it in England, when Wells and his band were in Europe as part of the 1966 American Folk Blues Festival package. Eric would usually announce that it was a Wells number when Cream performed it live, but it's actually a much older song. The earliest known version with that title—and, indeed, with more or less the same melody and structure—was recorded in Chicago, in July 1935, by Amos Easton, aka Bumble Bee Slim. The lyrics, though, are quite different.

Cream's normal arrangement of the song was similar to Wells's, and they cut a version of it at Atlantic. Eric usually sang it alone, but on this version he shared the vocal with Jack. It also featured several overdubbed guitar passages. This version remains unreleased, one of the "odds and ends" that wasn't in the warehouse fire.

Eric Clapton gets into the mood by playing an Albert King album during the *Disraeli Gears* sessions.
Photo by Don Paulsen

That same day they also cut a radically different version, considerably slower and showing the marked influence of Albert King in the guitar playing and arrangement. In fact, according to photographer Don Paulsen, Eric played several Albert King records on the studio record player, during the session, to get the feel right. The resultant version is the one that received posthumous release as the only studio track on *Live Cream*. It seems likely that this Albert King–style version was never used again—post–*Disraeli Gears* live versions reverted to the old Junior Wells arrangement—which isn't a surprise, because they put the new arrangement to a different use, thanks to the intervention of Felix.

"Also in the studio, along with Ahmet and Arif Mardin, was this very Italian-looking character," Ginger remembers, "who turned out to be Felix Pappalardi. Anyway, we did 'Hey Lawdy Mama' and played it back in the control room, and Felix said, 'Would you mind if I take the track home and take the vocal off?' So he took the track home and came back the next day with new lyrics. That was 'Strange Brew.'"

When Felix took the tape of "Hey Lawdy Mama" home with him that night, it was his wife, Gail Collins, who came up with new lyrics. Gail was, to say the least, something of a character in her own right.

One person who knew her well, albeit only in recent years, is guitarist Al Romano, who described her as "a brilliant woman who could read and write music and compose for and play just about any instrument." He also suggested that it was Gail who got Felix out of the folk clubs and convinced him that he could be a producer. Gail told Romano that the original title of "Strange Brew" was "Brain Stew," an interesting if bizarre concept, which Jack Bruce confirms. Gail also, allegedly, had something of a dark side, that intensified over the years as she and Felix got into serious drug use. As is fairly well known, she shot and killed Felix in 1983, during what most people believe was a domestic altercation. Despite extensive efforts, it's proved impossible to track her down. This may be because, according to Tom Dowd, she died sometime between 1991 and 1993. Others insist she is still alive, but none of them know her whereabouts.

The *Disraeli Gears* days were different times, though, and Gail's lyrics fit the era perfectly. Whereas "Hey Lawdy Mama" is about a big-legged woman about to leave her man, "Strange Brew"—with its references to "a witch of trouble in electric blue" and a "demon dusting in the flue"—is something else altogether. One curious rumor is that Gail was, or

at least believed herself to be, a witch. The possibility that the lyrics are, therefore, in some sense autobiographical and refer to Gail's relationship with Felix is very intriguing—but unproveable.

The new lyric was grafted onto the original backing track, albeit with new guitar overdubs (one of which Felix later claimed to have played), but the other parts remained the same. This still annoys Jack, who says, "I got really pissed off because we'd done the backing track for 'Hey Lawdy Mama,' and so, whoever it was, who shall remain nameless, said, 'Felix, take the backing track home and write a song over it.' So he came back with 'Strange Brew.' Fair enough. The only problem is that the bass line for 'Strange Brew' is different from the bass line for 'Hey Lawdy Mama.' So it still annoys me that it sounds like I'm playing the wrong bass line, because I'm playing the bass line for another tune."

Ginger and Eric going over the newly written "Strange Brew" lyrics in the Atlantic Studios with Ahmet and Felix. Where's Jack?
Photo by Don Paulsen

Although the "Strange Brew" lyrics were indeed grafted onto the backing track of the Albert King–style "Hey Lawdy Mama," it doesn't appear to be the same backing track as the "Hey Lawdy Mama" on *Live Cream*. But they may have recorded the Albert King–style "Hey Lawdy Mama" twice. It is not unthinkable by any means.

Despite the reservations about his own part, Jack is very complimentary about Eric's playing on "Strange Brew": "Yeah, 'Strange Brew' was a deliberate tribute to Albert King. But it was not a rip-off. That just wasn't the case. In those days, all of Eric's solos were statements, not just solos. All of his overdubs were amazing, I'd just sit there aghast."

With the completion of "Strange Brew" (and the Wells version of "Hey Lawdy Mama"), Cream seemed to have wrapped it up for the time being. Arguably, not a lot of finished material for a two-day session by 1967 standards, but much of the first day had obviously been taken up with the various disagreements over song selection—psychedelic hogwash versus straight-ahead blues. It's possible that Cream returned for a third or even a fourth day, but if they did, nothing was laid down after April 4 that was considered useable, since nothing was delivered to the library. More likely, they simply took a couple of days off before flying back to England.

EIGHT TRACKS
AND WAH-WAHS

Cream flew back to England on April 7, 1967.[1] During the month following Cream's return, they continued their rounds of the U.K. clubs. They
also put in an appearance at the *New Musical Express* poll winners concert, at what was then called The Empire Pool, Wembley. It was still a
marginally prestigious, but a totally anachronistic, event. They were per-
mitted to play two short numbers.

So whether the band or anybody else concerned remembers it this
way, Cream did indeed fly back to the States on or about Monday, May 8.
In keeping with Tom Dowd's story that Ahmet Ertegun rang him on a
Wednesday and told him that Cream would be in the next day, they presumably re-entered the Atlantic studios on Thursday the eleventh.

What is not known is the order the tracks were recorded in, but Jack
recalls the general scheme of things: "For the basic tracks on *Disraeli
Gears*, we only did one or two takes, but we'd often run through things
without the tape running. We didn't have a lot of time—not that it actually felt like that. Certainly Ginger and myself came from this background of
the worker musician. We did the Graham Bond Organisation's *Sound of*

---

1. This fact immediately throws into doubt a television appearance mentioned by at least one
    chronicler: on "Dee Time," an English television show, on April 6, they supposedly mimed
    to "Strange Brew," with a live vocal by Eric. "Dee Time" usually featured artists performing
    their latest hit single, whereas "Strange Brew" would not be released for over a month. More
    to the point, *Disc and Music Echo* listed the acts due to appear on that week's show, and
    Cream is not included. A later issue shows that Cream was booked for the May 22 show.
    The paper even states that they were to perform "Strange Brew." This May date is far more
    likely since the single had entered the charts the previous week.

65 album in three hours and thought that was normal. Anyway, the *Disraeli Gears* backing tracks were done fairly quickly. Then we'd hear them back and maybe do them again, but it wasn't like we'd spend all night on them. More time was spent on the overdubs, especially the guitar ones. Vocals I don't remember spending much time on at all. There was none of this dropping lines in that you can do today."

This speedy method of recording was indeed common, but was about to become obsolete. Once again, it was The Beatles who were leading the way. They had just finished *Sergeant Pepper's Lonely Hearts Club Band,* the product of several months' work in the studio. After its release that summer, self-respecting rock bands demanded more and more studio time—and sometimes got it.

The situation at Atlantic was more comfortable this time around. Jack remembers: "We were very fortunate to meet Tommy Dowd. What a fantastic engineer. And working with eight-track, that was a revelation. You ask anybody that's been in a studio, they say eight-track, that's the best sound. Once you get beyond that, you're always fighting to get back to the feeling of eight-track. And can you imagine us coming in there with our Marshall stacks and all of that? They'd never seen anything like it. But Tommy Dowd handled it very well."

Felix, too, was generous in his praise for Tom Dowd. He told *Hit Parader* in 1968, "Tommy is incredible. He's not the typical engineer. While I'm saying, 'the bass is a little fuzzy,' he'll turn around and say, 'Maybe that should be a 5/4 bar.' He's dynamite, and we listen to him a lot. It's the effort of five people in the studio, with no hang-ups at all."

Tom Dowd also devised a setup for the band that minimized leakage between tracks. He told Mark Cunningham, author of *Good Vibrations:* "I just made them feel comfortable and tried to keep them as far apart as I could. . . . They had Ginger in one portion of the room and I had the guitar and bass amplifier stacks positioned at 90° to where he was playing so that Jack and Eric could stand in front of their amps and still have eye contact with each other and Ginger. There was no need for earphones although ear protectors would have been a good idea 'cause they were so loud!"

Everyone also agrees that Felix was the perfect producer for the band. With their shared background in formal music, Jack and Felix were able to work out complex arrangements that Felix was able to quickly translate into recording terms. Jack says, "Felix was a great producer. He was able to get the best out of people without putting his own stamp on it. It was still very much what we wanted."

Although it wasn't released as a single until a year later, "Sunshine of Your Love" became, and remains, the most famous track on *Disraeli Gears.* It has been described as "the riff that launched a thousand bands" and "the birthplace of heavy metal." Jack modestly recalled, "That was a kind of magical riff. Not that I wrote it, it just appeared."

Of course, to all intents and purposes he *did* write it. As Pete Brown recalls: "Jack and I had been working all night, if not longer. Probably the second or third night in succession. We'd already done one good thing, but nothing was happening and I think we'd maybe had some sort of disagreement, which has been known to happen. Anyway, Jack suddenly grabbed his upright bass and said, 'What about this?' and he just played the riff of 'Sunshine.' And at that moment I looked out of the window, and it was getting light, and I sat down and started writing, 'It's getting near dawn, when lights close their tired eyes,' and all that stuff. And there it was. I wasn't there when the actual 'Sunshine of Your Love' hook was added, which I never actually liked."

"Sunshine" was certainly written, as were most of Pete and Jack's songs on the album, in the first three months of 1967. The two wrote quickly and in short bursts, because, as Pete says, "By that time there was no choice. There was no time to do anything but write quickly."

It is as impossible to precisely date the writing of the *Disraeli Gears* songs as it is to precisely date the recordings, but Eric came up with the following in a *Rolling Stone* interview in 1988, regarding a Hendrix concert at the Saville Theatre in London on January 29, 1967: "I don't think Jack had really taken [Hendrix] in before. . . . And when he did see it that night, after the gig, he went home and came up with the ['Sunshine'] riff. It was strictly a dedication to Jimi. And then we wrote a song on top of it." Leaving aside the fact that—apart from the hook—Pete and Jack wrote the song together at one sitting, the basic sentiment of what Clapton is saying may well be true, and the timing does fit. If it is true, did Hendrix somehow know, since he was wont to play the song himself occasionally? In January 1969, on the BBC's "Lulu Show," he went as far as to dedicate an impromptu instrumental version of the song to Cream, who had recently broken up.

One of Tom Dowd's favorite stories concerns the recording of "Sunshine." He recalls that "For the most part they'd run a song down, agree on it and say, 'Let's do it.' But on 'Sunshine,' Ginger had a problem with the drum concept. They ran it down several times, but they weren't happy with it. So I said to Ginger, 'Why don't you try the American Indian drum beat on it?' And he said, 'What's that?' And I said, jokingly, 'You obviously never saw any Westerns.' And I kind of chanted it for him, the DUM dum-dum-dum rhythm. He said, 'That's great,' and we made the record. The downbeat was where he was hitting the snare, and in rock and roll it normally goes two and four. So when he played the American Indian rhythm, it put the backbeat on the other beat, and it worked."

Tom's story has the ring of truth, but Jack has no memory of it and says, "That's just the way Ginger would have played it. I think we'd even done it live before we recorded it."

As, indeed, they had. There is an interesting tape that has recently surfaced in collectors' circles, from the Ricky Tick club in Hounslow, West London, that most probably dates from April 22, 1967, i.e., after their first trip to the United States but before the bulk of the album sessions. The band performs "Sunshine," but the drum pattern is quite different from the recorded version and, indeed, from all subsequent live versions.

What Jack does recall is the band's working out the end of the song. He says: "I remember Eric coming up with the chords for the turnaround at the end, which kind of finished it off—A, C, and G."

Tom Dowd feels that, apart from "Sunshine," most of the songs were, as he puts it, "road tested" before they were recorded. But in fact, very few of them were. Bearing in mind how quickly the album was recorded, it's a testament not only to the brilliance of the musicians, but also to the skill and imaginations of Felix and Tom. One must assume, however, that most, if not all, of the songs recorded in May were at least rehearsed in the U K , even if not actually played live, before Cream flew back to the States.

Jack and Pete's songs were fully scored, but this was not the case with several of the others, including "Tales of Brave Ulysses." According to Jack, "There was a guitar, bass, and drum part, which we sort of played together. But I improvised the melody line, which didn't exist. I didn't get a credit for that, but those are the breaks."

One of the most striking things about the recording of "Ulysses" is Eric's use of the wah-wah pedal, one of the earliest examples on record. Felix described how it came about in a 1968 *Hit Parader* article, and at the same time summed up his role as producer of the band. About "Tales of Brave Ulysses," he said, "I'm very proud of that. The Cream had all the words set and a good hold on the melody. That's what we started with. We ran it down a couple of times and took a break. Eric Clapton and I took a walk and ended up at Manny's instrument shop on 48th Street. They'd just got a bunch of Vox wah-wah pedals in, so we bought one. Now, it was difficult to think about the sound and concept of the tune when the melody was only half together, and there was no real form. It was a very free-spirited tune, so any calculation I did was spontaneous. I didn't sit down and figure out how much echo should go here, where the riffs should be played, or how much space should go between the vocal phrases. Eric said it better than I could. He said I was the doctor. All I do is juggle the things around and put something in that will fix it. As it turned out, the wah-wah was perfect for 'Ulysses.' It's just a matter of taste."

"No smiling, we're serious musicians creating art." Atlantic Studios during the *Disraeli Gears* sessions. PHOTO BY DON PAULSEN

The song itself, as mentioned earlier, resulted from the chance meeting of Eric and Martin Sharp. Eric now says: "He had the lyrics, and I had just got a very simple chord progression. But I was a stumbling songwriter, and I didn't have any knowledge of theory or how to go about it. To me, writing a song was a miracle. And I could probably come up with about one song a year in those days." Simple it may have been when Eric first conceived it, but by the time the band and Felix had worked it over, it had become a quite extraordinary piece—brooding, majestic, and full of atmosphere. Without doubt, it is one of the great songs of the '60s.

As for the lyrics, Martin Sharp remembers how they came about: "I went to Spain and then took the ferry to the island of Formentera, and on the way over someone pointed out this little island and said, 'That's where the sirens sang to Ulysses.'"

The opening lines are quite literal and refer to Martin getting away from the dreary London weather and escaping to warmer climes. However, the song quickly turns a little more abstract and poetic, but essentially, it's the story of Ulysses resisting seduction by the sirens. Martin admits that the song is also full of nostalgic memories of summers in Sydney. According to his friend Richard Neville, it is specifically about an old girlfriend, Anou. This seems quite likely, but after thirty years, Martin is genuinely not sure. He does say of the structure, however, that "I loved Judy Collins's version of 'Suzanne,' and that gave me the rhythm of the words."

Not only were few of the *Disraeli Gears* songs played live before being recorded, only a few made their way into the live act afterwards. "Sunshine" and "Ulysses," of course, were played quite often, but of the rest, only "We're Going Wrong" made it beyond a couple of performances.

"We're Going Wrong" is another song with an unusual structure, in that it doesn't follow the usual verse-chorus-verse structure. Rather, it relies on its shimmering texture and sheer intensity to succeed, not to mention Ginger's hypnotic repeating tom-tom pattern. Commenting on the song to *Rolling Stone* in 1968, Eric said, "You know that 'We're Going Wrong' was, in fact, made in two different keys, but we mixed them in such a way that it's not very noticeable—you're supposed to dig the over-all effect and atmosphere of the number, not the fact that it's in two different keys. I mean, it wouldn't work if you did notice it."

Curiously, it's the only song on the album that Jack wrote without Pete Brown. Jack says of its composition: "I was walking along Bracknell Gardens and just thought of it. It's a very simple piece, inspired by a Gil Evans number called, I think, 'Gone, Gone, Gone,' which has a similar chord progression. I'd probably just been listening to it. I also wrote the lyrics, such as they are. I don't often write lyrics, but when I do, the music and the lyrics happen at once. It was a personal statement. It was how I felt at the time."

Excellent though the *Disraeli Gears* recording is, the best recorded version of "We're Going Wrong" is probably the one they did for the BBC TV show "Twice a Fortnight," which was broadcast on November 26, 1967. That recording features not only one of Eric's most stinging guitar parts, but also one of Jack's most expressive and impassioned vocals. Fortunately, this version is available on the *Fresh Live Cream* video.

Jack also wrote a set of lyrics for "Take It Back," another of the tracks that was first recorded on the lost demo tape. Jack says, "It was about burning a draft card, and I had the line, 'Take it back, get that thing right out of here,' about receiving a draft card. And I gave it to Pete, for whom I have a lot of respect, but it got too artsy-fartsy for me. It could have been a good song for the time and struck more of a chord than it did."

Pete doesn't think it's too artsy-fartsy and isn't quite sure what Jack means. He'd also forgotten that Jack had the original idea, and thought the antiwar concept was his own: "It's a kind of anti-Vietnam song or anti-war song. It's about the draft or doing things for money, something you feel conscience-stricken about. The line, 'I've got this thing, got to keep it sharp. Won't go to places where it won't shine in the dark,' is about sexuality being destroyed by war. I think that's what I was trying to get at."

The song, at least as recorded, is deceptively lighthearted, and sounds quite vaudevillian. There are even hints of New Orleans jazz about it; one can almost imagine a trombone or a tuba in the background. Much of the party atmosphere was supplied by Jenny Dean, a famous New York groupie, and her friends, all whooping it up in the studio. Jack says of them, "They were very nice, I liked them." He also remembers spending his birthday, May 14, with Jenny in New York—further evidence of when the album was recorded.

At least one other person claims to have been on that session: Al Kooper, from The Blues Project. He recently said, "I played this really

rocking piano part on 'Take It Back' that got erased. Tom Dowd said it was an accident and was very embarrassed." Tom denies this hotly and claims that Al was never anywhere near the studio during the *Disraeli Gears* sessions. Jack isn't quite as sure. He also believes that Al didn't play but thinks that he might have come around to the studio, because they were friends by that time. Jack adds, "Anything on *Disraeli Gears* that has piano, I played it—including 'Blue Condition.'"

"Blue Condition" is Ginger's only composition on the album, and it's most people's least-favorite track. Slow to the point of plodding, Ginger doesn't so much sing the lyrics as intone them. It lacks even the weird humor of the later "Pressed Rat and Warthog." It isn't as though he couldn't

DISRAELI GEARS/CREAM

write good material. "Sweet Wine" is excellent as are "Those Were the Days" and "Passing the Time" from *Wheels of Fire.* Jack claims, however, that he and Felix had to completely arrange everything Ginger brought in, almost from scratch. It's difficult to see what they could have done with "Blue Condition," though. And oddly enough, Jack likes it.

The most interesting thing about "Blue Condition" is that the lyrics—Ginger's own—would appear to be an accurate reflection of his state of mind at the time. Seemingly, while Jack was having his crisis over the trouble getting his songs recorded, Ginger's own feelings regarding the songwriting/publishing credit situation were coming to a head. Ginger says: "Things were not going as I envisaged them or wanted them, and I was drinking quite heavily at the time and spending a lot of time in the bar downstairs from the studio."

It was in Martin's, the bar in question, that the idea for the other song that most Cream fans hate, "Mother's Lament," came up. Ginger relates the story of how they came to do it: "Eric and I used to do it for fun sometimes. We both come from similar backgrounds. My grandad used to sing these extraordinary music hall comic songs, but I think it was Eric who actually came up with 'Mother's Lament.' It was one of those songs that was obviously in both our genes. One of those songs you hear once and you know all the words."

Ginger goes on to describe how he and some drinking buddies began singing the song in Martin's one day: "We were in the bar and probably happily inebriated. The other people in the bar heard us singing it and, being Americans, it really appealed to them, this sort of cockney humor. They said, 'You've gotta record it,' and we were in a pretty happy state of mind, so we did. I don't regret it: I think it *is* rather funny."

Ginger's right; it is funny. And tucked away at the end of the album, it makes for an appropriately wacky coda to all the serious stuff. It's also one of the few examples of the humorous side of the band, something they originally intended to explore but dropped fairly quickly.

Disraeli Gears contains several tracks that, although among Cream's best, have somehow been overlooked. "World of Pain," the other Collins-Pappalardi-Clapton track, is a subtly restrained ballad, full of delicate touches. There is more wah-wah on this one, but instead of taking center stage, as it does on "Ulysses," it is skillfully blended with what is perhaps the best recorded example of Clapton employing what he refers to as his "woman tone" guitar sound. He described it to *Beat Instrumental* as "[A] sweet sound . . . more like the human voice than a guitar. You wouldn't think that it was a guitar for the first few passages. It calls for the correct use of distortion." Apparently, the sound is produced by removing all the treble from the tone controls and either turning up both pickups or using only the rhythm pickup.

Contrary to what Ginger seems to have thought, Jack was more than pleased to record material from other writers. Jack says, "It was nice when somebody came in with an idea that wasn't just a blues. Not that I don't love the blues. Things like 'Sitting on Top of the World' and 'Born Under a Bad Sign' were wonderful, but for someone to come in with a song like 'World of Pain,' that had interesting changes, was great."

"World of Pain" also features one of the best examples of Jack and Eric trading vocal sections, about which Jack says: "Eric had a lot of trouble with the vocal, because he wasn't really a confident singer at the time, although I always loved his voice. We just hammered it out in the studio."

Several writers have criticized "World of Pain"'s lyrics for being either simplistic or just plain silly—in particular the central image of a lone tree in the winter rain. Actually, it's a simple yet acute image; the tree's situation is analogous to the writer's feeling alienated by city life. The theme—a search for nourishment in desolate surroundings—is actually reminiscent of Betty Smith's novel *A Tree Grows in Brooklyn,* later a film classic directed by Elia Kazan. "World of Pain" is not great literature, perhaps, and may be a touch angst-ridden, but it is a creditable attempt to deal with an emotional and relevant topic.

The tree mentioned in the lyric, incidentally, was real. At the time, Felix and Gail were living in MacDougal Alley, a tiny mews of beautiful cottages and townhouses, located just off the 8th Street end of MacDougal Street, in the heart of Greenwich Village. There are, indeed, trees growing along it, most of them right up against the houses. According to Ginger's ex-wife, Liz, cab drivers could never find MacDougal Alley. She remembers being driven around Washington Square Park for what seemed like hours, by a cab driver who plainly believed she and Ginger had invented the address.

Eric about to do an overdub. Atlantic Studios during the *Disraeli Gears* sessions.
PHOTO BY DON PAULSEN

Jack has less-than-fond memories of the place. He recalls: "MacDougal Alley is very nice now, but it wasn't then, or at least their place wasn't. We were all invited there for a meal, and I remember going

into the kitchen, because I fancy myself as a bit of a cook. Gail was chopping vegetables, and there were literally hundreds of roaches crawling over everything."

One of the album's most underrated songs is Eric's version of Blind Joe Reynolds's "Outside Woman Blues." A simple twelve-bar blues it may be, but Cream's version really rocks along and the interplay between the three musicians is breathtaking. Eric's "woman tone" is again to the fore, and the recording has a marvelously dense sound that in no way conflicts with the song's sprightly quality.

Reynolds, the song's author, is a shadowy figure, known only to have been active as a musician in the Missisippi Delta between 1927 and 1931. Clearly, though, his musical life must have been longer than that. Only a handful of recordings, however, are definitely attributable to him, including "Married Woman Blues," "Third Street Woman Blues," and "Ninety-Nine Blues." "Outside Woman Blues" was cut at the Paramount studios, around November 1929, in Grafton, Wisconsin, where a number of Delta musicians were recorded. It was originally released on Paramount, but was re-released shortly afterwards by the budget Broadway label.

What's interesting, of course, is that this is the only real blues on the album. Although they were never strictly a blues band, the blues, or at least their version of it, was still a vital part of Cream's live set. Even the Bruce/Brown numbers like "SWLABR" and "Take It Back," which—on the basis of the Ryemuse demo versions—could have gone in a more bluesy direction, are given an almost pop flavor on *Disraeli Gears*.

The *Disraeli Gears* track with the oddest title is undoubtedly "SWLABR." It caused much debate at the time and, seemingly, it was ages before anybody writing about Cream actually listened to the lyrics and realized that "SWLABR" probably stood for "She Was Like A Bearded Rainbow" or, perhaps, "She Walks Like A Bearded Rainbow." Either way, it's certainly one of Pete Brown's more unusual lyrics, with lines like, "But the picture has a moustache," and later, "But the rainbow has a beard." Discussing the song, Pete says, "I think it was written around the same time as 'Sunshine' and yes, it's a very weird thing. I wouldn't write it now, or I'd write it in a different way. . . . I mean, the thing is that the male blues are very misogynistic, and a lot of people on the British blues scene were writing like that without really knowing what they were doing. They wouldn't today. I'm sure I wouldn't. 'She was like a bearded rainbow,' yeah, a bit dodgy."

Talking about "SWLABR," Jack came up with an astonishing revelation: "The music was definitely influenced by the Monkees. I don't really know why, something about the bridge, I think." At the time, the Monkees may have been one of the most successful acts in the world, but their highly commercial pop songs and teeny-bopper appeal were regarded as frivolous and culturally irrelevant to all right-thinking rock fans (most of whom had had a sense-of-humor bypass).

Monkee homage or not, it was another good song that never really made it into the live act. Another was "Dance the Night Away," which may have only been played once, at the Oxford May Ball, held May 27, 1967. If that was the only live version, it really is a shame, because "Dance the Night Away" is another classic, even if it doesn't immediately sound like Cream. The most obvious musical comparison is with The Byrds. According to Jack, this was no accident: "Yes, it's a deliberate tribute to them, and I asked Eric to play his twelve-string on it." At the time of the album's release, Eric told the *Record Mirror*, "We admire [The Byrds] tremendously as musicians, and they are also friends of ours. David Crosby, who left [The Byrds] recently, told us he likes the song very much."

The lyrics may well be Pete Brown's finest of the period and, uncharacteristically, reflect what was going on in his life—although the surreal quality of the lyrics was very much a reflection of the era. Pete says: "It was a very dreamlike time, made more so by my state of mind. Only dancing, and sometimes sex, kept me on the earth. Other times I felt in danger of literally floating off the planet, and I was quite frightened by it. The songs about dancing, 'Dance the Night Away' and to a lesser extent 'I Feel Free,' are about that. Those two and 'White Room' were exceptions. Usually my lyrics with Jack were not autobiographical, primarily because I was writing them for someone else to sing. That was mainly Jack, of course, and he had to feel comfortable singing them."

Disraeli Gears is one of those rare records where the whole is greater than the sum of its parts. What was created has a genuine unity, based not so much on a single musical style—Cream, after all, played in a variety of styles—but on a consistency of sound that relied heavily on Felix Pappalardi's production technique of stacking and layering the instrumental tracks, which was made possible by Atlantic's eight-track capabilities. It was an approach he would take to its logical conclusion on Cream's third album, *Wheels of Fire,* and was a considerable departure from, and improvement over, the production of *Fresh Cream.* Without taking anything away from the musicians or Jack's skills as a writer and arranger, the overall success of *Disraeli Gears* owes a great deal to the talents of Felix and, indeed, Tom Dowd.

Whether Pappalardi or Dowd should be regarded as fourth or fifth members of the band is a moot point. Their presence certainly made one thing abundantly clear: given the right surroundings and sympathetic coworkers, Cream could create material in the studio that was as good as, but intrinsically separate from, their live act. For whatever reason, few of *Disraeli Gears*'s songs made it into the live act, which, to a large extent, continued to be based on their version of the blues and their penchant for extended improvisations. Very little of either appear on *Disraeli Gears,* which is neither more nor less than a well thought-out collection of great songs. That the band, especially Eric, should find the album faintly embarrassing is not really surprising.

As Eric told *Melody Maker* at the time of its release in November 1967, "It's a good record, a great LP, but it was recorded last May, and it's not indicative of what we are doing now. When I hear it, I feel like I'm listening to another group. It's an LP of songs, and there's no extended improvisation . . . anywhere." Whether or not the band regarded *Disraeli Gears* as an aberration, they never recaptured the lightness of touch the album demonstrated, nor did they return to the brevity of its songs.

If *Fresh Cream* was blues-based and *Wheels of Fire* would be a superior example of the "new rock," then *Disraeli Gears* was the band's psychedelic pop album. It's undoubtedly serious in intent and immaculately performed, but it completely lacks the gratuitous heavy riffs and misapplied classical influences that were soon to bedevil rock and that gave birth to the Deep Purple/Yes school of pomposity.

Despite Cream's reputation as the putative fathers of heavy metal, *Disraeli Gears,* instead, should be compared with other 1967 classics— like Pink Floyd's *Piper at the Gates of Dawn* or the early singles by The Move and Traffic—where well-crafted and imaginative songs were all-important. Arguably, though, the long delay in the release of *Disraeli Gears* militated against such comparisons. The world was moving fast in 1967,

Jack and Felix contemplate a quick jam. Atlantic Studios during the *Disraeli Gears* sessions.
PHOTO BY DON PAULSEN

DISRAELI GEARS/CREAM

and by the time of the album's release at the end of the year, tastes were shifting, and *Disraeli Gears* was regarded in hard-core underground circles as not only a pale reflection of Cream's live act, but also as lacking overt musical complexity and social commitment.

Before leaving the *Disraeli Gears* sessions, one final mystery should be mentioned. In the middle of the tape logs, between the entries for "World of Pain" and "Take It Back," is an entry for something called "I Can't Forget." It is clearly labeled as a Cream track. But nobody questioned about it has any recollection of a song with that title. Or, as Jack pithily put it: "'I Can't Forget'? No, I don't remember."

Whatever it was, it wasn't a lost Bruce/Brown classic, although another Pappalardi/Collins song is a possibility. Jack thinks it might be an old blues, but if so, it wasn't one that Cream performed live, because he's sure he would remember it. That it's an alternate working title for a known track is not possible either, because all the album's other songs are accounted for in the log, and a run-through wouldn't have been deposited in the library.

There are yet other possibilities. Jack mentioned that he and Felix jammed extensively in the studio, but as far as he remembers the tapes were never running—but maybe on one occasion they were. Another theory is a second music hall sing along à la "Mother's Lament," which, if true, the group was wise to leave in the can. One per album is enough. This leaves one last possibility: a cataloging error. That would mean "I Can't Forget" is not a Cream recording at all. Joey Helgara, the current head of the Atlantic tape library, thinks this is unlikely and argues that his predecessors were "pretty efficient." But as a Cream fan himself, this may be wishful thinking. Needless to say, no tape exists, and if it ever did, it was more than likely destroyed in the big fire.

THE PEAK OF THE
MOUNTAIN

Although they had briefly played in America and had cut a fine new album, not a lot had changed for Cream. The Murray the K show had been a local success at best, and it would be fully six months before the world got to hear the complete results of their endeavors at Atlantic.

On a more positive note, *Fresh Cream* had finally been released in the States and was starting to garner the band some good notices, primarily in the underground press, and some radio play on FM stations. If their reputation was beginning to build in America in May 1967, back in England, the band was largely unaware of it.

At the end of May, a single from the Atlantic sessions was released—"Strange Brew" backed with "Tales of Brave Ulysses." By then, "Strange Brew" was nearly two months old. By contrast, "Ulysses" had only been finished some two weeks earlier. But releasing a record that quickly was by no means uncommon, especially if the record company— the English one anyway—had been been waiting nearly six months for the follow-up to a hit single. The band wasn't that happy with the choice of A-side. Clapton told *Disc and Music Echo,* "We would have liked ['Tales of Brave Ulysses'] . . . to have been the top side. But everybody said no, the top side wasn't very good, but it was commercial. So we gave in."

Reviews of the single were favorable without being ecstatic. An interesting one was by Jimi Hendrix, who was the "Blind Date" singles reviewer in the June 10 issue of

One of the era's more unlikely gigs: "Barbeque '67" at the Tulip Bulb Auction Hall, Spalding, Lincolnshire. A tape of Cream's performance exists somewhere.
AUTHOR'S COLLECTION

Melody Maker. The idea was for a celebrity to be played a batch of new singles without being told what they were, at least until they had made an opening, and frequently embarrassing, comment on each one. More often than not, the reviewer would guess the wrong artist and unwittingly rubbish their "best friend's" latest work. Hendrix made no such faux pas in the case of Cream, and said of "Strange Brew," "I know who that is all right, by the first note. Ooh that's nice. I like this record because I like the way [Clapton] plays anyway. His solo is just like a guitar player in the South named Albert King."

As Hendrix predicted, the "kiddies," as he referred to them in the review, didn't go for the record, not in huge quantities, anyway. It reached a creditable, but not staggering, number 17 on the U.K. chart and failed to break into the Billboard top 40 in the States. "I Feel Free" had peaked at number 11 in the U.K. and failed to chart in the States. Whether "Strange Brew" was a worthy successor to "I Feel Free" is moot. "I Feel Free" was undoubtedly a stronger and more compelling release, but if anything, the softer-sounding "Strange Brew" is, in modern parlance, more radio friendly. The group's labels Reaction and Atlantic would have had every reason to believe that it would do as well, if not better, than their first hit.

"Sunshine of Your Love" might have been a better choice and might have broken them in America earlier, but in the end it was academic. Cream would be in the vanguard of bands who no longer needed a hit single to succeed. Despite that, several U.K. rock acts, like Jethro Tull, Deep Purple, and Atomic Rooster, persevered with releasing singles in their native country, if not in America, well into the next decade.

Over the next month or so, reports appeared in the English pop press that Cream's new album was due for imminent release. At that time it was to be entitled, somewhat prosaically, "Cream." Then on July 29, the *Record Mirror* reported that it was now renamed *Disraeli Gears* and would be released at the end of August 1967. At least they got the new album's name right.

The origin of the album's name is well known, but Ginger recalls the full story: "We had this Austin Westminster, and Mick Turner, who was one of our roadies, was driving, and Eric was talking about getting a racing bicycle. It was a beautiful day, and we were driving around Richmond Park and talking about bicycles and gears and things. Mick went, 'Oh

yeah, *Disraeli gears,*' meaning Derailleur gears. We all just fell over. It was so funny that we said, 'That's got to be the album title.'"

One of the minor mysteries surrounding *Disraeli Gears* is why it took so long to be released. Although never satisfactorily explained, part of the reason has to be the exotic cover that finally graced the record. This was no record company in-house overnight rush job.

By the time of the late July press release announcing the new title, the cover photographs had already been taken by Eric's friend and Pheasantry neighbor, Bob Whitaker. Whitaker was another Australian, but he'd moved to England earlier than Martin Sharp, after having met and photographed The Beatles on their Australasian tour in 1964. Sometime in early July 1967, Bob was invited up to Scotland to join Cream, who was on tour there. The idea was to photograph the band in full hippie regalia. This was, after all, the "Summer of Love."

It didn't quite work out that way, though it did produce one of Jack's fondest memories of Cream. He recalls: "We played in Inverness, in a cinema. And I said OK, let's climb Ben Nevis [the highest mountain in

Eric: "It didn't seem so high at the bottom." Ginger: "Neither did we!" Jack, Ginger, and Eric climbing Ben Nevis, Scotland, summer 1967.
PHOTO BY ROBERT WHITAKER

Scotland] and so we did. We climbed beyond the tree line, which is not bad going in high-heeled boots and velvet capes. We were up there when the mist came down. We were going through the mist—we'd got to the snow line by this time—and there's all these climbers with ice picks and crampons and everything. And this guy said, 'Oh my god, it's The Cream. Can we have your autograph?'"

In theory, they were looking for location shots for the album cover. Their mountaineering activities, however, are more explicable by the fact that they were all tripping on acid. It certainly accounts for what they did next. "And then we actually ran down Ben Nevis," Jack continues. "There was Eric, Ginger, Charlotte, and me, and we started running, and if you've ever run down Ben Nevis you'll know it's not a good idea because you can't stop. So we sort of ran down, going faster and faster, and then sort of ran up into Fort William and into a cake shop and started eating all these cream cakes. And I think that the best part, really, is that the photographer forgot to put film in his camera, so we had to go back to Regent's Park [in London] and sort of pretend it was Ben Nevis for the album cover."

To be fair to Bob Whitaker, he did take several photographs of the band next to a Scottish mountain, though it might not be Ben Nevis. In any case, Bob's carefully posed shots of the band and Charlotte Martin, al fresco, were about to be desecrated by Martin Sharp in the name of art.

At some point that summer, Eric asked Martin Sharp to design the sleeve for *Disraeli Gears*. Seemingly, he left Martin with an advance tape of the album and instructions to do anything he wanted. Martin recalls: "Previously, I had traced material from books, but then I thought, I may as well cut up the books, it's easier. So for *Disraeli Gears,* I cut up Bob's contact sheets along with images and designs from various sources and put a basic collage together, over which I used the paints. I tried to capture the sound of the music in the cover, that warm flurescent sound, so I worked with florescent paints. I used a lot of old books on decoration. I think the wings are from [Albrecht] Dürer, but I have no idea where most of the other images came from. I think that the African chief came from a *National Geographic* magazine, and the tap probably came from an old Army & Navy Store catalog. I just did the artwork the same size as the album cover and sent it off."

The end result was perhaps the most striking album cover of the '60s, a period noted for elaborate and overtly artistic album sleeves. Bands were no longer satisfied with promo shots of themselves leaning against cars and began insisting on covers that mirrored their increasingly complex music. In England, pop artist Peter Blake became an overnight celebrity after producing The Beatles' *Sergeant Pepper* cover, and photographer Michael Cooper broke new ground with his 3-D photo for the cover of the Stones' *Their Satanic Majesties Request.*

Not surprisingly, many bands commissioned pyschedelic poster artists to execute not only their album sleeves, but also posters and other items of promotional material. In the States, the leading San Francisco artists—Rick Griffin, Victor Moscoso, and Stanley Mouse—worked directly with bands like The Grateful Dead and Steve Miller, while in England, the artists' studio known as Hapshash and the Colored Coat produced sleeves and posters for The Who and The Incredible String Band, among others. Much of the work by all of these artists is stunning and completely evocative of the era. No single piece, though, is as strik-

Cream contemplate becoming a quartet. Scotland, summer 1967.
Photo by Robert Whitaker

ing as Sharp's cover for *Disraeli Gears.* It's so vibrant and rich in detail that it almost defies description, and the overused term "psychedelic" fails to do it justice.

The front cover's central image is a tight head shot of the band (taken by Whitaker), hovering over what might be a female figure from a ship's prow, underneath whom the words *Disraeli Gears* are emblazoned—all of which appear to be supported by a series of Greek columns. Between the two Dürer wings is the single word "Cream." Surrounding these images are pieces of baroque ornamentation, flowers, a tap, a pocket watch, and much more. Around the border are Martin's trademark zigzag lines and bubbles. The whole image, including the photo, is overlayed in florescent paints, mainly pink, with some orange and green.

The back cover is marginally less successful, though still extraordinary. The central image here is a close-up photo of an open human eye. Arranged in a circular pattern around it are cut-up photos of the band (all taken by Whitaker) and a few other characters, including Superman and an African chief, plus a figure known as the nude over Jerimiah, from Michelangelo's Sistine Chapel ceiling. Between the photos, and sometimes on them, are many flowers, which seem to be hand drawn. There is also a photo of a Chelsea street on both edges that recedes into the background. In comparison to the front cover, the back's use of florescent paint is restrained and confined mainly to the flowers and the lime-green sky.

Does the cover mean anything? Is it hiding a deep underlying symbolism? According to Martin the answer is no, but as he says, "I've been much more conscious of my imagery since then. I never thought [*Disraeli Gears*] was that good, but I guess that it's my best-known work." And then he adds, laughing, "I think artists should get royalties for album sleeves."

Sharp, of course, went on to design sleeves for *Wheels of Fire* and for the first album by Ginger Baker's Airforce. In 1967, he also produced some of the finest English psychedelic posters, including the classic Bob Dylan poster "Blowin' in the Mind," and "Sunshine Superman," a Donovan poster printed on silver foil. By the end of the '60s, Martin had returned to Sydney, where he still lives. He still paints, but his main preoccupation is the work of Tiny Tim, for whose musical estate Martin is the executor. Martin's fascination with Tiny Tim dates back to 1967, when he

"They shall not pass." Eric Clapton, Scotland, summer 1967.
PHOTO BY ROBERT WHITAKER

was introduced to Tiny by Eric Clapton, and as he points out, the royalties from "Ulysses" frequently paid for Tiny Tim's recording sessions!

The summer of 1967 was the golden era for Cream, both artistically and emotionally. Ginger's dream of a totally cooperative unit came as close as it ever would to being achieved, given the personalities and histories of those involved. As Eric says: "From a distance you could see the going up and coming down. . . . There was a period, and I'm afraid it is associated with a drug. . . . We were introduced to, and started to take a lot of, LSD. That was around the time of *Disraeli Gears,* shortly after [the recording], when we were touring Scotland. . . . That was the peak of the mountain, when we were so together and so tight, and we loved one another so much, and we just never spent a minute apart." According to Eric the band was so close that few outsiders could penetrate their self-imposed energy field, and they unconsciously invented a group language that no one else could understand.

Leaving aside Eric's understandable hyperbole and the natural association of Scotland and mountains, an incredible bond had indeed developed among them, and this confidence and energy naturally carried over into their music. But they needed more suitable venues than cinemas in small Scottish towns in which to ply their trade.

So much had happened over the previous year, both in the music world and in youth culture, that neither Robert Stigwood nor the band, for that matter, could ignore it any longer. Cream had eschewed the English underground completely and never played at trendsetting clubs like UFO or Middle Earth.[1] But even the most blinkered and old-fashioned of managers could hardly have failed to notice that the real action had shifted to the West Coast of America, especially San Francisco. Even then, Stigwood nearly blew the band's chances of breaking into what was obviously their natural market. He rejected an offer for them to play at the Monterey Pop Festival in June 1967. Monterey Pop, and the film that resulted from it, launched the careers of an array of new artists, like Janis Joplin, Jimi Hendrix, and Jefferson Airplane, and put the new counterculture firmly on the map.

"[Stigwood] didn't tell us that we'd been invited, which pissed me off," Eric recalls. "He told us after he turned them down [but] he said, 'I

---

1. Incidentally, a poster advertising a Cream gig at UFO in July 1967 is a recent fake.

have a reason for that, I want to break you in San Francisco independent of this festival, so that you have more of an impact.' And I don't know if that was good thinking or not. I've given up worrying about that."

In some ways, San Francisco was an unlikely setting for a new musical and social movement. A small city by American standards, San Francisco had long been viewed, with more than a little condescension, as a small cultural outpost on the otherwise artistically barren western edge of America. The traditional view, extending back over a century, was that new trends come from Europe, gain a foothold in New York, and eventually work their way west. The exception to that rule of thumb was of course black music and culture, which originated in the South but spread to the northern cities, notably Chicago. There was a degree of surprise then when San Francisco began attracting national, and later international, attention as the center of a new counterculture.

Closer examination reveals that the Bay Area was actually a very likely location for such a social revolution. Although the city fathers had rarely condoned it, San Francisco had been host to radical and bohemian activities going back to the mid-nineteenth century. San Francisco had tolerated and nourished, in varying degrees, anarchists, socialists, poets, and just plain eccentrics as long as anybody could remember. In the late '50s the city's North Beach neighborhood had been home to an extensive beatnik community, based around poet Lawrence Ferlinghetti's famous City Lights Bookstore and any number of coffee houses.

As the '50s gave way to the '60s, the Beat ideal waned, and North Beach became as famous for its strip clubs as for its coffee houses. But by 1964, a new community was growing up in the Haight-Ashbury district, a few miles from North Beach, on the edge of Golden Gate Park. At the time, it was a blue-collar neighborhood that had seen better days but was full of beautiful Victorian houses with cheap rents. The first "new" inhabitants of the Haight-Ashbury were students or dropouts from nearby San Francisco State College, along with refugees from North Beach, like poet Michael McClure. But unlike the Beats, who were into jazz and poetry, this new group were post-Beatles rock kids. And although the Beats had smoked dope and experimented with exotic drugs, the new generation had discovered the "wonder drug," LSD.

By the end of 1965 America had, in the Haight-Ashbury, its first fully fledged hippie community. And despite attempts by the authorities to condemn it and the supposedly degenerate lifestyle of its members, it became a magnet to ever-increasing numbers of young people reacting against the materialism of the age, the Vietnam War, or simply their parents.

In the early post-Beat days, folk music had boomed in San Francisco, as it had elsewhere in the States. But, with the arrival of The Beatles and the Stones in 1964, that changed almost overnight. Previously serious folkies plugged in and began playing electric rock and roll. In San Francisco, many of these newly electrified musicians were already living in, or soon moved to, the Haight-Ashbury. By the end of 1965 the neighborhood was home to bands with exotic names like Big Brother and the Holding Company, The Charlatans, and The Great Society. Not everybody could make music, though many tried, but the music soon became—along, perhaps, with the sex and the dope—the most visible and definable facet of the scene.

It soon became apparent that venues for the new music were required, and by early 1966 the city's music scene had two focal points, the Avalon Ballroom, run by Chet Helms's Family Dog organization, and the Fillmore Auditorium, run by Bill Graham.

The two venues shared several things in common: both were dance halls rather than seated theaters, both featured liquid light shows (the colorful bubbling and oozing oil and water projections that all but obscured the performers), both came to use psychedelic posters to advertise their shows, and both featured the new style of acid-rock bands. The attempt was to create something new, a total environment that reflected or enhanced the experience of an acid trip—something that Graham always attempted to deny, or at least play down. For Helms it was, more or less, his raison d'être.

For various reasons, Graham was able to book bigger names—or at least exotic British bands, who inevitably cost more than local heroes like The Grateful Dead. It was Graham, then, rather than Helms, who booked Cream into his ballroom for an extended run between August 22 and September 3. As Clapton said, they may have been better off if they'd played at Monterey, but as it turned out, playing the Fillmore was a defining moment for the band. Whether by luck or judgment, by playing in San Francisco in the summer of 1967, they'd plugged straight into the motherload. It was the first step in turning them into counterculture superstars, a concept that should, surely, have been an oxymoron.

As Eric now says: "[The Fillmore] was the right place at the right time. There was definitely nothing else like it, and we fit in perfectly. . . . We loved it. It was like coming home. And we used to stay out in Sausalito, across the bay, and it was just what we wanted. [I] made tons of friends. People that seemed to have the same philosophy. It was the time of my life."

Jack says of the Fillmore: "The place was crammed. I think we played there for ten days, something like that. And I think we were blown away by the fact that people knew who we were. [It also] had the best sound system we'd ever used up to that point, which was crucial." A month after the Fillmore gigs, Jack told the *Village Voice* that he'd played the best music of his life in San Francisco.

At the time, Eric was very taken with all the community activities in San Francisco, like the Dead's free concerts in the park. As far as is known, Cream never played anywhere for free—it's hard to imagine Ginger or Stigwood agreeing to it, although Ginger and Eric's post-Cream band, Blind Faith, made their only U.K. appearance at a free concert in London's Hyde Park.

On the whole, though, Eric was less than impressed with most of the local bands. He now says of them: "As much as I saw of the bands that were killing them there—I mean Big Brother and the Jefferson Airplane—I was very unimpressed. . . . I was shocked at how many people weren't aware of what they had on their doorstep. The only thing I saw [that I liked], apart from the obvious blues greats, was Paul Butterfield and his band. They were fantastic."

To some extent, Eric's reservations are understandable. Cream were dedicated musicians with a tightness and virtuosity that most bands could only dream of. Several of the English bands following in Cream's wake, like the Jeff Beck Group and Fleetwood Mac, while lacking the combined abilities of Cream, also were predicated on musical excellence. At the same time, one feels that Clapton missed the point, somewhat, of what the San Francisco bands were about; their shambolic looseness was part of their charm. And to suggest that the local musicians and audience were unaware of black music, particularly the blues, is mistaken. Interestingly though, Cream had an enormous influence on the local bands, most of whom were looking for a way to break out of folk-rock or simple blues riffs. Within weeks of Cream's appearance, the Jefferson

Airplane, in particular, were playing louder, heavier, and far more experimental music.

If Cream was an influence on the local bands, the Fillmore had an immediate influence on Cream. As legend has it, Cream arrived with their stock set-list comprising an hour-long show, but came to realize that, at the Fillmore, they were expected to play much longer. More than that, the crowd response was overwhelming; they shouted to Cream that they should play whatever they wanted, for as long as they wanted—the number of songs wasn't as important as the length and elaborateness of the improvisations. To some extent the legend is true. The band was flattered by the audience reaction and was only too pleased to demonstrate their musical virtuosity, but whether they started playing sets of a far longer duration is doubtful. More likely they simply reduced their playlist and extended the solos.

Sadly, no official or in-house soundboard recordings were made of these shows. There exists, however, a poor quality audience tape from the night of September 3, which features, apart from a very free-form "Sweet Wine," an unusual, possibly unique version of "Spoonful." Instead of Clapton's usual dazzling barrage of blues riffs, ancient and modern, he plays his entire solo as something closer to an Indian raga.

Clapton suggests that the blues offered an open pathway for improvisation: "I think the blues is easiest to work with [in order] to go somewhere else or to jam for any length of time. For instance, 'I'm So Glad' is more or less in one key, and 'Spoonful' is only in one key. There are hints of chord changes, but they're not really stated."

Jack is more specific, and probably more musicologically accurate: "It's obviously true that some of our songs were easier to improvise on than others. You could [improvise] on songs like 'Spoonful,' 'NSU,' and 'I'm So Glad' because of their modal quality. Although we didn't talk about it, I think that's what it was. You couldn't improvise lengthily on something like 'Deserted Cities of the Heart,' because it was too structured. Nor could you on a twelve-bar blues, because there's a limit on how many choruses you can play unless you're Paul Gonsalves. [Gonsalves was the tenor sax player with the Duke Ellington Orchestra]."

Technically speaking, modal music refers to virtually any style of music that does not conform to normal Western diatonic scales. The term usually refers to Arabian or Eastern music (including the Indian Raga), which uses non-Western scales. Confusingly, the term also refers to numerous folk songs from the British Isles, and some black American blues, where the music is based on "modal chords." A modal chord is one where the third note of the scale is removed, giving the chord a harsher quality.

It is possible, however, that Jack means "unstructured," rather than modal, i.e., a song that has no formal, repeating structure. This lack of formal structure means that the musician does not have to return to a fixed point every specified number of bars—twelve in the case of a standard blues—which makes the tune ideal for open-ended jamming. Such an unstructured song might utilize major, minor, or, indeed, modal chords.

The band had become so used to playing structured sets in England that the freedom was exhilarating. After all, wasn't freeing themselves from the constraints of playing strict twelve-bar blues or three-minute pop songs part of the basis of Cream's existence? They knew they had the ability to do it, and the urge to do so must have been enormous. They took the chance, and the era of Cream as the world's premier jamming rock band was born. This was not the band that had recorded *Disraeli Gears*. If a dichotomy had existed in May between their live set and the collection of tight, concise songs on *Disraeli Gears,* it had suddenly become a yawning void.

To this day, opinion is divided as to whether this "new" Cream was a good thing. Some suggest that regardless of how well Cream performed, the long solos were inherently boring, not to say grossly self-indulgent, and the band should have concentrated on working the more concise *Disraeli Gears* songs, like "SWALBR" or "Dance the Night Away"—and other originals—into the live act. A second body of opinion has it that, right up until their demise in October 1968, their live performances were utterly sublime. The third view, and the one held to a large extent by the band, is that playing long improvised versions of their songs worked for a while, but probably not much longer than the first American tour, which finished in the middle of October 1967.

Eric's own view was summed up in an interview in *Hit Parader,* conducted around October 1967, but not published until early 1968: "We don't do anything straight. We're into music much more now—as much as jazz musicians are into music. There are no arrangements except for arrival and departure points. Sometimes we just play free for half an hour." Clearly, he was still enjoying his newfound musical freedom.

Despite the obvious changes in Cream's playing style on the first U.S. tour, at least as manifested in the extended solos, their basic set-list had barely altered since their inception. Only "Sunshine of Your Love," "Tales of Brave Ulysses," and, occasionally, "We're Going Wrong," of the *Disraeli Gears* songs, had been added to the act. There is no real explanation for why the act changed so little, beyond the obvious fact that constant touring gave them little time to rehearse new material. It may also have been that they wanted to continue along the improvisational path, and that, with the exception of "Sunshine"— which could easily run to ten minutes when played live—none of the *Disraeli Gears* songs lent themselves to extended soloing.

Even so, it is difficult to imagine Jack resisting the idea of the band performing his, and Pete Brown's, other *Disraeli Gears* songs— "SWLABR," "Dance the Night Away," and "Take It Back"—if Eric and Ginger had really wanted to include them. For the most part the set continued to revolve around their usual blues covers like "Spoonful," "I'm So Glad," and "Rollin' and Tumblin'," along with a smattering of originals like "Sleepy Time Time," "Sweet Wine," "NSU," and the omnipresent "Toad."

In one sense the lack of new material was academic, because most audiences on the first U.S. tour were hearing the material for the first time. Arguably, the appearance of *Disraeli Gears* during the tour would have confused the audience, not only for the obvious reason that the album lacked the long solos for which the band had rapidly become known, but also because it would have been full of material the band was not playing. Such confusion is exactly what did happen when the album was finally issued. It's possible that the band was aware of the possibilty and deliberately held the album back until after the tour had finished. More likely it was held back because no one had yet realized the importance of releasing an album at the start of a tour.

Nowadays—or indeed, at any time since about 1970—the idea of "getting the album out for the tour" is paramount, but back then things were different. No one knew how big the rock market was going to become, and all the methods that record company publicity and promotion departments later devised to service the growing number of counter-

culture outlets simply did not exist. The audiences and the bands knew that albums were now far more important than singles. It took a while for the record companies to catch up.

Ad for the Whisky a Go Go gig, September 1967.
BARRY GRUBER COLLECTION

In any event, that first tour following the Fillmore dates was a wonderful period for the band. For once they found themselves booked, for the most part, into appropriate venues. Their audiences not only loved the music but also looked like and shared a philosophy of life similar to theirs. One has the feeling, though, that Eric's view of the hippie life was a tad rosy, as if he expected that Haight-Ashbury was going to be full of people like his friends in Chelsea. Instead, by the time Cream arrived there, the place was full of sixteen-year-old runaways. His view of L.A., the band's second stop on the tour, is more understandable: "From the very first time we went there, I didn't know what [L.A.] was all about, any more than I do today. It all seemed to be cardboard to me, and all they had [then] was the Whisky a Go-Go. More than anything else, it was drugs there. There was a very strong feeling of drug orientation in the music . . . [especially] strong hallucinogenics. And as much as San Francisco was branded with that, I found it was much more prevalent in L.A."

Curiously, on that first L.A. visit, Eric was interviewed by an underground rock paper, *World Countdown.* He told them that Cream had just had a wonderful time in San Francisco playing for The Family Dog, the Fillmore's chief rival. Of course, they'd actually played the Fillmore—which begs several questions about Eric's state of mind that day.

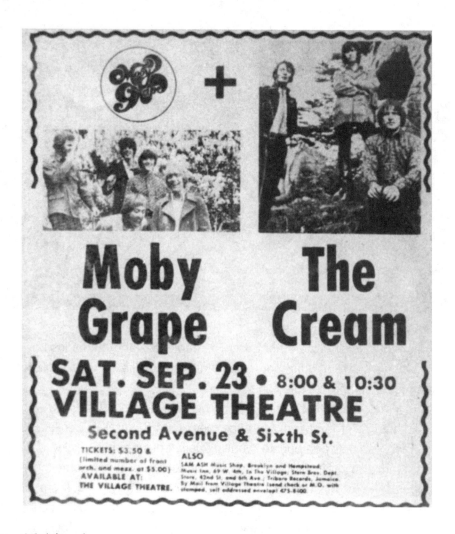

Moby Grape + The Cream
SAT. SEP. 23 • 8:00 & 10:30
VILLAGE THEATRE
Second Avenue & Sixth St.

TICKETS: $3.50 &
(limited number of front
orch. and mezz. at $5.00)
AVAILABLE AT:
THE VILLAGE THEATRE.

ALSO
SAM ASH Music Shop, Brooklyn and Hempstead;
Music Inn, 69 W. 4th, In The Village; Stern Bros. Dept.
Store, 42nd St. and 6th Ave.; Tribore Records, Jamaica.
By Mail from Village Theatre (send check or M.O. with
stamped, self addressed envelop) 475-8400.

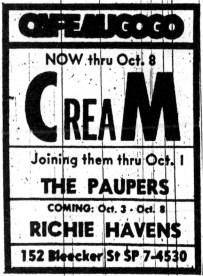

CAFE AU GO GO
NOW thru Oct. 8
CREAM
Joining them thru Oct. 1
THE PAUPERS
COMING: Oct. 3 - Oct. 8
RICHIE HAVENS
152 Bleecker St SP 7-4530

After playing in L.A., the band headed for the East Coast, playing Boston before their return to New York. Their New York area debut on this tour was somewhat less prestigious than has been previously reported. The band played two nights at The Action House in Long Beach, Long Island, on September 22 and 24. A witness to one of the shows estimates the crowd at about fifty people. On September 23, Cream made their first Manhattan appearance since Murray the K, at the Village Theater on Second Avenue, on the Lower East Side.

This beautiful old Loew's theatre was to become the Fillmore East in March 1968, when Bill Graham took it over. At the time, however, a different promoter was using

it, and was, as Pete Townshend so poetically put it, "something of a piss-hole." Allegedly, the promoter paid scant regard to the sound system, the lights, or the requirements of band or audience. Nonetheless, the audience response was overwhelming, and Cream was quickly booked again for the following Saturday—by which time they were in the middle of a twelve-day run at the tiny Cafe Au Go Go, on Bleecker Street. They probably started a little later at the Au Go Go that night. In any case, Bleecker Street would have only just been coming alive when they finished their set at the Village Theater, around midnight.

Eric onstage at the Cafe Au Go Go, NYC, October 1967.
Photo by Don Paulsen

Cream was well received at the Au Go Go, and an excellent review of their opening night, the 26th, appeared in *Billboard.* The reviewer states that "the trio thunders toward musical destruction at high amplification, tearing down all preconceived musical ideas, ideals, and forms, but building, at the same time, a series of melodic structures, each self-contained but connected as a song."

The writer singled out "We're Going Wrong" as the best song of the night: "The structure of the song hinges on several steps of music. Bruce, working the bass almost as a lead instrument, was topped by Clapton, who used feedback to produce a continuous musical pattern for each step. Baker was the driver setting the pace. After a takeoff . . . Bruce wrapped up the lyric, then the music was brought up higher and higher until wipeout." Whether this reworking of the song was unique is not known. Clearly, though, it was a radical departure from the *Disraeli Gears* arrangement. Interestingly, the few extant live versions from 1968 adhere quite closely to the one on the album.

Though most people who attended the Au Go Go shows shared *Billboard*'s positive reaction, several patrons complained that Cream was playing loud enough for a baseball stadium. From here on, it was only going to get louder.

After New York, the band moved on to Detroit to play at The Grande Ballroom, the venue that became their mid-America stronghold. Eric says of the place, "[It] was very much the same thing [as the Fillmore], and I was surprised, really, at being in the middle of America . . . that it was very sophisticated in terms of being up to date with San Francisco."

Detroit had evolved its own underground community that was quite distinct from the one in San Francisco. Detroit is an essentially blue-collar town, based around its automotive industry, which was still thriving in

DISRAELI GEARS/CREAM

Cafe Au Go Go, NYC,
October 1967.
PHOTO BY DON PAULSEN

the '60s. It had few of the artistic and bohemian traditions of San Francisco, and while Detroit's hippies shared certain things in common with their brethren in the Bay Area—notably a fondness for sex, drugs, and rock and roll—they were, of necessity, tougher and far more militant. If the hippies thought they were given a hard time by the authorities in San Francisco, they would have not believed Detroit, where the situation was ten times worse. Detroit hippies felt constantly under siege and, consequently, had little time for the "peace and love" ethic.

Musically, Detroit was famous for Motown, but it had a white music scene as well, and the locals had a fondness for hard-driving rock. Not surprisingly, therefore, the local underground bands were disdainful of what they perceived as the wimpy folk-rock and blues played by most of the San Francisco bands. The local music heroes, in particular the MC5 and The Stooges, were avant-garde in their own way, mixing rock and roll with the free jazz of Albert Ayler and John Coltrane. The MC5 also added a revolutionary tinge to the music, and were founder members of the White Panther party.

The local music scene centered on the Grande Ballroom, which opened in the fall of 1966 under the auspices of Russ Gibb, who'd received advice from, and the blessing of, Bill Graham. For the first year he booked only local bands, but by the summer of 1967, when profits started to improve, he started booking big-name acts, including touring British bands like Cream. It seems that the MC5 was less than impressed with Cream, not so much because of their music, but by their supposed lack of missionary zeal. Despite the English trio's fondness for illicit substances and fornication, they were certainly not into doing either "in the streets"—a concept that, in theory, at least, formed part of the MC5's revolutionary platform.

Cream played their first series of gigs at the Grande over the weekend of October 13 through 15, and the MC5's reservations notwithstanding, it was a major success for both the band and the ballroom. Writer Ben Edmonds attended the shows, and recalled them, as part of an article on the Detroit scene in the '60s, for *Off the Wall* magazine in 1993. "The appearance of Cream in mid-October was a watershed weekend. The ballroom was jammed well beyond legal capacity, the shows were magnificently performed and rapturously received. It was an engagement that was talked about for months afterwards, and Cream soon rivalled the Beatles and the Stones in local popularity. In the space of seventy-two hours the Grande went from being a place to *The* place."

For Cream it was not just a pleasure playing at the Grande. Their triumph in Detroit meant that they had a foothold in the heartland of America—a vital part of their bid for nationwide success.

Jack onstage at the Cafe Au Go Go, NYC, October 1967.
PHOTO BY DON PAULSEN

ONE GOOD NIGHT IN FOUR

Cream returned to England in mid-October 1967, flushed with success and a burning desire to return to the States for the appreciative audiences and big bucks. *Disraeli Gears* was finally released at the end of the month, but, not surprisingly, the band was less than enthusiastic about it; it now bore even less resemblance to their live act than it had when it was recorded six months earlier. And they'd written several new songs they were anxious to record.

The reviews of the album were mixed—ranging from cautious to favorable. *Melody Maker,* loyal from Cream's inception, was the most positive. Under the heading "The Creation of Pure Energy from The Cream," the reviewer states, "With this new album the Cream step up a gear. Not a giant step from the first album, *Fresh Cream,* but neverthless a more quality-heavy package of incredible Cream super-power." The review goes on to liken Eric's guitar playing to a menacing machine gun, which reaches "serpent-like deep into the Cream's varied and hypnotic musical journeys." He concludes with the opinion that "this is the creation of pure energy—from the top, the centre, the bottom, all the way through—the Cream." Hmm. Well, at least they liked it.

The English magazine *Beat Instrumental* also liked the album but avoided *Melody Maker*'s pur-

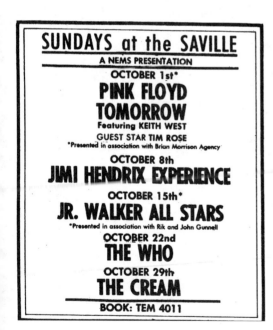

SUNDAYS at the SAVILLE
A NEMS PRESENTATION
OCTOBER 1st*
PINK FLOYD
TOMORROW
Featuring KEITH WEST
GUEST STAR TIM ROSE
*Presented in association with Brian Morrison Agency
OCTOBER 8th
JIMI HENDRIX EXPERIENCE
OCTOBER 15th*
JR. WALKER ALL STARS
*Presented in association with Rik and John Gunnell
OCTOBER 22nd
THE WHO
OCTOBER 29th
THE CREAM
BOOK: TEM 4011

ple prose. They refer to Eric "twisting minds with his beautiful playing," and to Ginger playing the drums "as if his life depended on it." They add that Jack was singing as well as ever. Too well, they suggest, to be compared with any blues singer in the country. Overall they describe the album as "brilliant."

Rolling Stone was a little more reserved. The review starts off quite effusively: "Within the grooves of this record are miles of listening pleasure. Eric Clapton, Jack Bruce and Ginger Baker are simply superb musicians with the gift of unending virtuosity." But the reviewer then seems to reverse himself and indicates that, in his opinion, the album doesn't hang together and is marred by several weak songs. Among these he includes not only "Blue Condition," which might have been expected but, more surprisingly, "Dance the Night Away" and "We're Going Wrong." He certainly likes "Sunshine" and seems to like "Ulysses." He groups them with "Outside Woman Blues" and makes the odd comment that "the listener has no choice but to stand in awe of their precision, grace and exquisite sense of time." It's almost as though he wished that the listener did, indeed, have a choice.

On the whole, he likes the album, especially the production and the increased musical sophistication over *Fresh Cream.* A mixed review, then, but the last halfway decent one Cream would receive in *Rolling Stone* during the band's lifetime. It should be pointed out, though, that at this time *Rolling Stone* was little more than six months old and had yet to become the accepted arbiter of taste in all matters rock.

Billboard gave the album a good review, predicting that it would be "another giant" for the band, whose music they describe as "wall to wall rock"—whatever that means—"tinged with blues and 'flower' lyrics."

Cheetah magazine was not kind at all. The reviewer trashes the band's instrumental abilities and concludes by saying, "What their style lacks most is rhythmic drive; their rhythms are accurate and square—in other words they're very English—and that's death to blues playing." It was a harbinger of bad reviews to come.

In the end neither mixed reviews, nor the band's own misgivings about *Disraeli Gears,* made much difference. Their continued popularity in the U.K. ensured a number 5 slot on the album charts at home (one higher than *Fresh Cream* had reached), while their sudden rise to fame in the States during their summer/fall 1967 tour resulted in the album reaching number four in America. By contrast, *Fresh Cream* never rose above number 39.

As the band members were quick to point out, they'd come a long way since the recording of *Disraeli Gears,* and they had new material that they wanted to record as quickly as possible. Quite what style of album they wanted to record is open to debate. Clearly, they wanted to record something that was closer to their live act than *Disraeli Gears* had been, and, presumably, with longer cuts, but they obviously had aspirations well beyond that simple goal. If nothing else, working with Felix on *Disraeli Gears* had shown them what could be achieved in a studio. With *Fresh Cream* they had already attempted a simple transfer of the live act into the studio and, successful as that attempt had been, doing that and nothing more would have been a waste of talent and technology. Equally, to produce a collection of short songs, however wonderful they may have been individually (as were most of the *Disraeli Gears* cuts), was not what the band wanted either. In other words, the band was confronted with its perennial live/studio dichotomy.

In retrospect, *Disraeli Gears* managed to combine Cream's gravitas and virtuosity with a degree of wit and panache, but it's easy to see that in a rock world that was, by late 1967, tossing all things frivolous and psychedelic out of the window, that the album could be viewed as somehow lightweight. For many fans "Mother's Lament" was a bad joke; "Take It Back" was vaudeville, not blues; and there was simply not enough screaming guitar on the album. The band had similar reservations: for them it was an an album of mostly good songs, but with nowhere near enough extended playing on it. In consequence, any new studio material from Cream was going to be heavier—and a good deal more serious.

This new approach was reinforced in November 1967, when Clapton told *Melody Maker,* in an article entitled "Cream Declare War on Singles": "I'm a great believer in the theory that singles will become obsolete and LPs will take their place. . . . To get any good music in a space of two or three minutes requires working to a formula, and that part of the pop field leaves me cold. I hate all that running around trying to get a hit." Clapton's one proviso was that if they happened to record anything during an album session that was short enough and sufficiently commercial, they would consider releasing it as a single. This was an option they exercised when they issued the engaging, but eccentric, "Anyone for Tennis" (a *Wheels of Fire* outtake) in May 1968. It may have been the right length, but it certainly wasn't commercial, only reaching number 40 in England, and failing to dent the top 40 at all in the States.

If nothing else, the band's "no singles" policy shows just how powerful Cream had become, and how removed they were from the band that cut *Disraeli Gears* and two top 40 hits. Few artists at the time had the clout to dictate terms of this sort, to either their record company or management, neither of whom could have been happy about the new policy. They would certainly have wanted Cream—as well as all their other acts—to record songs specifically aimed at the singles market. It was a measure of the changes taking place in the rock world that Cream was able to get away with it. Power was shifting to the artists for the first time.

marquee
90 Wardour Street | London W.1

Thursday, November 23rd (7.30-11.0)
★LONG JOHN BALDRY
★THE NITE PEOPLE

Friday, November 24th (7.30-11.0)
BLUES NIGHT
★PETER GREEN'S ★FLEETWOOD MAC
★THE BLACK CAT BONES

Saturday, November 25th (8.0-11.30)
★NEAT CHANGE
★ HERBAL MIXTURE

Sunday, November 26th — CLOSED

Monday, November 27th (7.30-11.0)
★ THE NICE
★ THE SENSORY ARMADA

Tuesday, November 28th (7.30-11.0)
★THE CREAM
★ REMO FOUR

Wednesday, Nov. 29th (7.30-11.0)
★ STUDENTS ONLY NIGHT

marquee studios • 4 Track • Stereo • Mono • Recordings
10 Richmond Mews, W.1. 01-437 6731

Ad for one of Cream's last U.K. club dates, The Marquee, London, November 1967.
BARRY GRUBER COLLECTION

Of course, whatever Cream did or did not record could not stop their record companies from releasing album tracks as singles, which Atco did most successfully in February 1968, when "Sunshine of Your Love" reached number 5 in the States—the highest position Cream achieved in the singles chart on either side of the Atlantic. ("Sunshine" wasn't released as a single in the U.K. until September 1968, when it only reached number 25.)

In terms of recording, albums were now Cream's primary focus, and they returned to Atlantic—by now their studio of choice—as early as their touring schedule allowed. The earliest confirmed sessions for *Wheels of Fire* took place at Atlantic in early October, when, according to the studio log, they completed two numbers: "Sitting on Top of the World" (usually

DISRAELI GEARS/CREAM

credited to Chester "Howlin' Wolf" Burnett, but actually dating from the '20s and a recording by the Mississippi Sheiks, and possibly written by Sheiks member Bo Carter) and Albert King's "Born Under a Bad Sign," both of which ended up on *Wheels of Fire.* In interviews earlier that summer, both Felix and the band stated that they envisioned adding a horn section on record. But without consulting them, someone at Atlantic overdubbed King Curtis–style horns on "Born Under a Bad Sign." It was a good idea, but the execution was poor, and all parties rejected it. Ironically, this version was another of the "odds and ends" that escaped the early '70s warehouse fire.

Significantly, the band was only two songs into the new album and it already had more overt blues on it than *Disraeli Gears.* More important, both "Sitting on Top of the World," and "Born Under a Bad Sign" are performed with much more solemnity than "Outside Woman Blues," the token blues on *Disraeli Gears,* which by comparison is positively buoyant and lighthearted.

With the band touring so much, recording dates had to be fitted in wherever possible. The October sessions at Atlantic were feasible only because of the band's residency at the Cafe Au Go Go. The next idea was to block-book the Atlantic New York studio for mid-December, between tours. Unfortunately, the band was unaware that Aretha Franklin had already booked time over part of the same period, and Cream only managed a couple of days in the studio before she arrived. The screwup gave Eric the opportunity to go overdub a solo on December 16 for Aretha on "Good to Me as I Am to You," one of the highlights of what became the *Lady Soul* album.

In the end, the studio segment of what became *Wheels of Fire* was completed at Atlantic over a ten-day period, in mid-February 1968. It's an understatement to say that the newly recorded material made an even greater use than *Disraeli Gears* of the studio facilities and of the combined talents of Felix and Jack. It may well have the densest sound and most complex mix of any rock album from the era. Many of the innovative production techniques employed on *Wheels of Fire* rapidly became industry norms. Ginger's drums, previously confined to one channel, crisscross the stereo arc, as do several of Eric's guitar overdubs, most noticeably on "Politician." Panning instruments from one channel to the other would become a cliché within a year.

The production style is based partly on ideas and influences, particularly from classical music, that were only hinted at on *Disraeli Gears*. Apparently, Felix's favorite technique was to combine the ever-present underlying drone from Middle Eastern music with a variation of Bach's notion of playing overlapping notes to create the illusion of more than one instrument.

Where it's most obvious is in the stacking of the various overdubs, notably on the opening of "White Room," which was created by mixing multitracked violas, played by Felix, with two very high strings on Eric's guitar. That opening remains one of the most distinctive in rock and leads into the best-known track on the album. Later edited and released as a single—though never conceived as such—it reached number 9 in the States in October 1968, just as the band was breaking up. Not released until January 1969 in the U.K., it only reached number 28.

Ironically, "White Room" is another Bruce-Brown song that was initially unappreciated, and Jack had to persuade the other band members and Ahmet Ertegun of its worth. It was probably one of the songs that Ahmet dismissed as "psychedelic hogwash" at the *Disraeli Gears* sessions.

As with *Disraeli Gears,* only a handful of tracks from *Wheels of Fire* made it into the live set on a regular basis. In fact, as far as is known, only "White Room" and "Deserted Cities of the Heart" (of the originals) made it to the stage, and then only on the farewell tour, although they occasionally used the instrumental part of "Passing the Time" as the intro to "Toad."

Unlike *Disraeli Gears,* however, where virtually all the tracks could have been played on stage without radically altering them, several tracks on *Wheels of Fire* must have been written solely with the studio in mind. Notable among these is Jack and Pete's "As You Said," which features only Jack and Ginger—Jack on acoustic guitar, cello, and vocals and Ginger on high hat. It's the only acoustic number Cream ever performed, but to achieve the desired effect, Jack was overdubbed more than five times.

Like the lyrics of *Disraeli Gears, Wheels of Fire*'s lyrics are as engrossing as its music. Pete Brown says of their collaborations of this period: "Jack's a very visual composer. Those songs are like tone poems. You can really see the imagery. Jack's also a romantic writer—I mean 'romantic' in the nineteenth-century sense—and in some of the best things we wrote together, I was really motivated by his romantic style. I was putting his musical images into words and relating them slightly to myself, so I could make it more convincing. Jack has always said that he doesn't care about the words, as long as they sound all right. To which I say, 'pooh!'"

Ginger's songs on *Wheels of Fire,* written in collaboration with Mike Taylor—another musician with a jazz and classical background—are also "romantic," both musically and lyrically. They are also a considerable improvement over the lugubrious "Blue Condition." Like many of the Bruce-Brown songs, the Baker-Taylor lyrics are full of nostalgia for different or simpler times. In fact almost all of the lyrics of the original songs on *Wheels of Fire* are about nostalgia, loss, or regret. Even the covers, "Born Under a Bad Sign" and "Sitting on Top of the World," are hardly light-hearted or optimistic.

Is it fair, therefore, to relate the nature of the lyrics, and to an extent, the nature of the music, to the band's state of mind at the time? We now know that they were already feeling the strain of constant touring and that the problem of song credits remained unresolved, allowing resentment to grow. The temptation, then, is to say that because the band was miserable and frustrated, it spilled over into the album and, taking the argument to its logical conclusion, that *Wheels of Fire* was a statement, albeit unconscious, of their imminent demise.

Needless to say, you can't do that. Aside from any other consideration, most of the lyrics came from outside sources. Therefore, if the lyrics apply to anybody, they apply, principally, to Pete Brown, but not to the band. In any case, the lyrics of *Disraeli Gears,* for the most part, are also unhappy, pessimistic, or full of regret and longing: "We're Going Wrong," "World of Pain," "Tales of Brave Ulysses," and "Blue Condition," being only the most obvious examples. It's really a question of musical context: on *Disraeli Gears,* Cream achieved a delicate balance of light and shade that was somehow lost on *Wheels of Fire.* By contrast, *Wheels of Fire* has an overall melancholic quality that does not make for easy listening. You have to be in the right mood to play *Wheels of Fire:* this is by no means a value judgment; few of the great works in music history could be described as everyday listening. Ironically, whatever the band's intentions may have been, *Wheels of Fire,* like *Disraeli Gears,* is still an album of songs, none of which is over five minutes long—short by the standards of their live performances. Clearly, another approach was required to get all facets of Cream's music on record.

Even before the Fillmore watershed, it had been obvious that however wonderful Cream's studio recordings were in their own right, they could only demonstrate a part of what the band was about. As Jack says, "Cream was like two bands: there was a studio band, where we had the ability to overdub, and there was the live band. Some of the [studio] things worked very well live, but some things were very difficult to realize live with only three people. . . . It was a problem that caused friction [within] the band."

The seemingly obvious answer to this problem was a live album, or better still, a double album, half live and half studio, which is what *Wheels of Fire* became. Both Felix and the band had been pressing for just that since they'd resumed recording in the fall of 1967. In fact, they'd been discussing the possibility of a live album among themselves since the recording of *Disraeli Gears,* which, whatever intrinsic merits it may have had, did not represent the live act at all. It took a while for Cream's English and American record companies to be convinced, after which it took even more time to arrange for any live recording to be done. It finally happened in March 1968, in Cream's U.S. stronghold, San Francisco. The idea was to record all the shows during the latter half of their two-week series of shows in the city.

In early 1969, Felix wrote in *Hit Parader:* "We rented recording equipment from a studio in L.A., and it was driven to the Fillmore in a giant Hertz truck. The truck was all decked out inside with two eight-track machines, a full console, and four speakers. Tommy Dowd was present, but the engineer for this session was Bill Halverson, a very young, incredible guy. Tom and Bill carefully set up all the mikes on stage and made preparations. I don't think the audience even knew [it] was going on."

DISRAELI GEARS/CREAM

Felix goes on to say that they didn't miss a note and that they "taped everything for five shows." But this doesn't make sense. If he means "shows" (i.e., complete nights), there would be four of them: March 7 through 10. If he means "sets" rather than shows, there should be eight of them, because there were two per night. (The band followed the Fillmore/Winterland norm of playing two sets, per night, for the same audience.)

Just to confuse matters further, the Atlantic tape log makes reference to seven sets, the missing one being the second set on the night of March 8. It seems that the missing tape never found its way to the library, but whether this was because of a technical problem or because it was lost or stolen before it arrived is impossible to tell. In any case it's academic. The only extant tapes of releaseable quality (and this applies to the

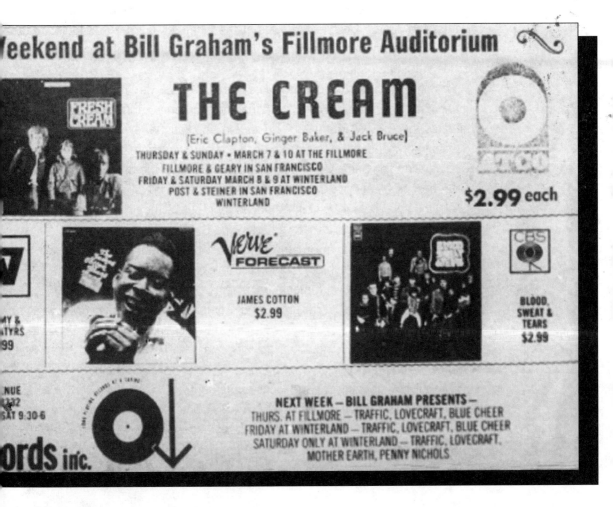

shows recorded on the last tour as well) are the ones that were issued in the '60s. The rest went up in smoke in the warehouse fire.

There are, however, some lo-fi tapes—probably rough mixes—from some of the shows that were recorded in 1968. One track from these reels, "Sunshine of Your Love," has been officially released (see discography) but because of the poor sound quality, it's unlikely that any more will be released. Before these tapes were returned to Polygram, who own the Cream catalog, several bootlegs were compiled from them, notably, *Live Cream Vol. 3,* which contains tracks from the October 4, 1968, show at the Oakland Coliseum.

On March 7, the band played at the Fillmore Auditorium, not Fillmore West, as is frequently assumed. Graham didn't move to the new premises until the following June. It was, in fact, the only night they played at the Fillmore that week. The rest of the shows were at Graham's larger Winterland Arena. Despite the "Live at the Fillmore" tag on the album, only "Toad" came from the Fillmore Auditorium. The rest were recorded at the Winterland shows.

Some feel that the *Wheels of Fire* live recordings were made too late in the band's performing career, and that the spontaneity and passion had already gone. By March 1968, frustration and fatigue levels had risen considerably, and there is no doubt that recordings from the first tour would have been better. As Jack told *Hit Parader* after the band had split, "The best of Cream live was never captured on record. We were at our peak when we did our first big American tour, but by the time they could get [it] together to record [us] we had slipped over the peak."

But the members of Cream were professionals, and as long as they weren't at each other's throats, they were able to put on a good show. The chief criticism of the live material on *Wheels of Fire* is that all of it, with the exception of Eric's dynamic and compact reworking of Robert Johnson's "Crossroads" (not edited, despite the legend to the contrary), sprawls unmercifully. And it has to be said that however much one approves, in principle, of Cream improvising at length, much of the album's live material drags and lacks excitement.

One reason may well be Felix's flawed vision of the album. He wrote in *Hit Parader,* "[I] knew I wanted numbers that spotlighted each guy as a soloist, but I could only get 'Traintime' and 'Toad.'" In choosing "Traintime" (solo harmonica) and "Toad" (Ginger's drum epic)—numbers that worked best in the context of an entire show—Felix filled up half the live disk with material that completely ignored Cream's main strength: their ensemble playing. That still leaves "Spoonful," which has some spectacular moments, when all three musicians mesh, but overall it lacks inspiration and drive. The problem, ironically, is Eric's guitar playing, which too often sounds like retreads of his favorite blues phrases rather than free-flowing spontaneity. By his own admission, his playing could sometimes be like this.

He now says: "We were all soloists, but I took it upon myself to think that I was the soloist. And I found that I was running out of ideas a lot of the time, repeating myself." It was a problem that would get worse. The irony is that they could still play together quite brilliantly. Based on material from these same shows, like "NSU" and "Sweet Wine"—which appeared after the band's breakup on the two *Live Cream* albums— Pappalardi could have put together something that better represented Cream's collective talents, and would have made for an album that still holds up today. As it turned out, the *Wheels of Fire* live disk, as issued, laid the band wide open to accusations of self-indulgence, something that no British band, at least, had ever been accused of before. The American critics were tougher on the band than the British in this respect. Probably the ultimate put-down came in Jon Landau's review of *Wheels of Fire* in *Eye* magazine. He describes Cream as being "for people who enjoy watching show-offs." Justified or not, that perception of the band is the primary factor that has stood in the way of a balanced assessment of Cream through the years. What tends to be remembered is sixteen minutes of "Toad," not an album of concise and melodic songs like *Disraeli Gears*.

One problem that got worse over this period was volume. Playing in bigger and bigger places meant that Jack and Eric kept cranking it up. Apart from the sheer noise level, the distortion also got worse.

For Ginger it became a nightmare: "Instead of having [just one] bass speaker and one guitar speaker either side of me, it suddenly grew into these huge double stacks. It got severely painful, and my pleas to turn it down were greeted with, 'No man, you're crazy.'" He also points out that the drums weren't miked, and people kept telling him that the only time they could hear him was during his solo. Ginger reckons that the problem got so bad that it was one of the factors that led to his ultimate disen-

PINNACLE

JEFFERSON AIRPLANE FEB 23-24
THE CREAM MAR 15-16 SHRINE
DANCE CONCERTS WITH OTHERS TO BE ANNOUNCED

Ad for Cream's appearance
at the Shrine Auditorium,
L.A., March 1968.
BARRY GRUBER
COLLECTION

chantment with the band. "It goes beyond the balance of logic," he continues. "If you keep turning it up, and everything is at maximum volume, and then you add drums, you end up with just this cacophony, and you damage your ears. [I] would get off a gig and think, 'Fuck it, I can't take it again, I can't do it another time.'"

Jack has a different view of the sound problem and blames it, largely, on the lousy house PAs they had to work with: "I mean, I did ask Ginger: 'Couldn't we get a proper PA? Maybe we could afford it now.' But he said, 'No!' Because Ginger was never into sound. He thought that sound was something you produced on stage, and that was it. He didn't realize that there was the possibility of sound reinforcement, sound enhancement, that could have done great things for us."

The spring 1968 tour kept getting longer and longer, with obvious deleterious effects. Curiously, despite his frustration over the noise, it was Ginger who continued to push them to play more dates. In a way, it wasn't surprising—their fees had gone up to a guarantee of $20,000 per gig, with a percentage of the gate on top. With a big crowd, it could mean upwards of $60,000—a far cry from the £40 per night that Ginger had demanded at the beginning. With hindsight, Ginger admits, however, that it got out of hand: "I think it would have been a good idea to have said, 'OK, we're gonna take a month here and just go on holiday' . . . but we didn't do that. We just kept on working."

By the end of April 1968, when they were barely halfway through the tour, they'd decided between themselves that the band would break up,

DISRAELI GEARS/CREAM

probably by the end of the year. The news, however, wasn't made official until July, after the tour had finished. The reasons for the breakup seem obvious now: the constant touring, the disputes over the songwriting credits, and Jack's frustrations over Ginger and Eric's lack of enthusiasm for his original material. The overwhelming thing, though, was that they'd created a monster. What had begun at the Fillmore as a spontaneous experiment in musical freedom began to oppress them. Jack says: "It was very like The Who having to destroy their equipment every night. . . . We had to play these long solos. That was the double-edged sword that did us in."

Eric is more specific. He now says: "In the early days [the long solos] became our strongest point. . . . Even someone like Leonard Bernstein was known to comment that [Cream's jazz-rock fusion] was like the first thing of its nature. . . . But it was all unintentional and, at the time it was born, it was all very exciting to know that we could [take the music] to this other place. . . . But I think where we lost out was when that's all it became, and it ran out of steam."

Clapton is of the opinion that on that second U.S. tour they played one good night for every four mediocre ones. He explains that "It was because you can't be that inspired for that long without going back to the fountain, going back to the spring, and working on the foundation of the thing. . . . It got to a point where I couldn't take it anymore. And the way that worked was that I heard The Band [an advance copy of the *Big Pink* album]. They did something that I liked better [than Cream], and instead of saying, 'Let's learn

Very psychedelic ad for Cream's appearance at the Electric Factory, Philadelphia, April 1968.

Somewhere in America, May 1968. But where exactly?
BARRY GRUBER
COLLECTION

Ad for Cream's appearance at the Island Gardens, West Hempstead, Long Island, June 1968.
BARRY GRUBER
COLLECTION

from this,' I just said, 'I don't want to do this anymore.' And I ran away, really."

In retrospect it seems ironic that a band that recorded the bulk of its studio albums in days, rather than in weeks or months, was unable to discipline its live excesses. The band's inabilty to reconcile these two polar opposites played a major part in its demise.

124   DISRAELI GEARS/CREAM

WHAT A BRING DOWN

After a long break over the summer, Cream's farewell tour began on October 4 at the Alameda County Coliseum, in Oakland, California. The show was one of four on the tour that were apparently taped by Atlantic, although the library tape logs are, for once, somewhat sketchy on the details. Seemingly, three cuts from this show, "Politician," "White Room," and "Deserted Cities of The Heart," showed up on the posthumous album *Live Cream Vol. 2.*

As it unfolded, the tour became a gruelling experience for the entire band. Eric remembers very little about it. He now says: "It's almost like a blackout for me—the ending of the band. Because I know we went through a whole long farewell procedure, but I don't remember."

Ginger, in contrast, remembers it all too well: "[It was] murder from my own personal view. You could go onstage and have a really bad night and be really unhappy about it, and yet we'd still get this incredible adulation. It didn't help, especially when you're not getting on personally."

The end was certainly unpleasant, though few fans realized it. Jack recalls: "It was difficult to be friends [with the other two] by the time we knew that the band was going to finish. Everybody had their own little group of friends, got to gigs separately, and so on. We were still doing it in a professional way; we were doing the gigs, but it just didn't have that joy that we had in the early days. Our hearts weren't in it anymore."

Jack knows exactly which night was the nadir for him: "It was when we played Madison Square Garden [on November 2] and we were playing on the revolving stage. I realized that I'd gone so far away from what I thought music was about. . . . I felt like a boxer, I felt that I should have been in the blue corner. I didn't feel like a musician anymore, I felt like an object. I just didn't really want to know anymore." Ironic, then, that the Madison Square Garden gig was chosen as the night when the band was presented with the award for the first album ever to go platinum. *Wheels of Fire* had already made over two million dollars.

The tour ended two days later. Then, following a three-week gap, they played their last shows on November 26. Suitably, they returned to London, the city of Cream's birth. British fans were predictably outraged, though, that not only had they not seen them for nearly a year, but the band had the gall to play only two shows—and only in the capital—to end their career. Cream later made the rather lame excuse that they didn't realize how popular they were at home.

How good the shows were depends on what reviews you read or who, from the audience, you talk to. Most people say that it wasn't a stunning show musically, but the atmosphere was extraordinarily emotional. The *Farewell Cream* film, shot that night, is of no real help in gauging the performance. Badly photographed, with terrible sound and far too many fast zooms and tight shots of the musicians' knuckles and noses, it has rightly been condemned by critics and fans alike. Ginger claims that Eric was furious with the director, Tony Palmer, for not using the best bits. Ginger also maintains that Palmer simply didn't know what the best bits were.

Before they actually broke up, the band had decided they would produce a final album. The original plan was to do another *Wheels of Fire*–style double album: half studio, half live. It's doubtful, however, that they had the energy or will to carry it off. It ended up as a single album, a hastily thrown together mix of live material from the farewell tour, and three newly recorded studio tracks, titled *Goodbye*. The album does contain some excellent material, notably Clapton's terse yet melodic "Badge," which, along with Jack's more experimental material like "As You Said," might have suggested new directions for the band if they'd stuck it out. The other two songs—"What a Bring Down," Ginger's cockney-inflected ironic comment on the band's breakup, and "Doin' That Scrapyard Thing," Jack and Pete's humorous take on Jack's childhood—while not the band's finest, have held up well. Even the live material has its moments, and is actually more exciting than most of the live portion of

Wheels of Fire. Unfortunately, the rag-bag nature of the record only points up its inconsistencies, and it falls far short of their best work.

At the time of *Goodbye*'s release in early 1969, Jack told *Hit Parader,* with only a hint of irony, "I like the album. Not [that] it contains the best music that ever happened, but because it reminds me of what it was like to be a star." These days he's more objective: "I think that was a kind of disappointing, half-hearted record, but . . . the band was over, and we did the best we could. I think 'Badge' is a great song. I think the other [studio] songs aren't so good, but I think it would have been better to have done a whole studio record as opposed to this kind of hybrid thing."

Many thousands of words have been written in attempt to sum up Cream's achievements and influence. Like so much rock criticism, the viewpoints depend entirely on who's doing the writing. Yes, Cream probably were pioneers of heavy metal as popularized by Led Zeppelin and a host of less-talented groups. Yes, the classical overtones in their work may well have spawned a lot of progressive or art rock (most notably Queen). And yes, the jamming style of Cream's later live performances probably did inspire members of the jazz fraternity to attempt a jazz/rock fusion. But there really is no way to be objective or definitive about the results of such influence, real or imagined, so no judgment will be passed here. What one can say is that Cream opened a door through which others followed. And in any field of artistic endeavor, finding a door and opening it is always commendable, irrespective of where those who follow choose to go.

Whether Cream succeeded in what they set out to do is another matter. Eric's well-worn comment that Cream amounted to "a few good licks" hurt both fans and the other two musicians. It was palpably untrue, and Eric seems to have softened that view in recent years.

Ginger has always shown unequivocal belief in Cream's achievements. He says, "We all had that incredible confidence, and we were enjoying it. We all sincerely believed we were the cream [de la crème]. I certainly thought I was the best drummer in the world. [We had] that attitude when we went to America for that first tour, like 'Yeah, sure, let's show those Yanks how to play.' That was our thing, you know. Anyone who was on the bill with us didn't stand a hope, because, 'Man, we can play'— like, 'cop this.' That's what it was about. [Cream] produced four fantastic records and created an enormous effect on the whole of the musical world." Baker's is an understandable if not particularly objective view, ignoring as it does the problem of Cream's live excesses.

Jack is considerably more reticent: "Ginger says that we all thought we were the best, and even Eric says that he didn't reckon any of the San Francisco bands. But I don't remember it like that at all. I remember being really insecure. I never thought we were that good, and I don't think the other two were that different—I may be wrong. But I was very proud of the band and, on a good night, it could be amazing." He is also, rightly, very proud of the Bruce/Brown catalog of songs that were, under duress or otherwise, recorded by Cream.

It's that aspect of Cream, the body of songs written primarily by Bruce and Brown, that is their true legacy. In the studio, most particularly on *Disraeli Gears,* they proved, unequivocally, that they were able to produce concise, dramatic, and melodic material that was the equal of any '60s band. It's quite possible that if they had produced a live recording earlier in their career that conclusion would have to be extended to include it. Unfortunately, as a live band they have to be judged on their later performances, which demonstrate only too clearly that the criticisms of self-indulgence were justified. It's a sad irony that it was that very self-indulgence that proved to be their most lasting influence on the rock world, particularly on musicians, and not the songs on *Disraeli Gears*—the bass riff on "Sunshine of Your Love" notwithstanding.

Almost as profound an influence was the notion of the "supergroup." Cream was essentially the first band that was deliberately put together based on each of the players' respect for each other as musicians. On paper this was a great idea: what could be better than a group of equally talented musicians, where every note of every instrument could be savored, and the interplay between the musicians be marvelled at? The problem is that gifted musicians have notoriously large egos; in performance they will try and upstage each other, and offstage minor squabbles can turn into major disputes. That Cream sidestepped the worst of those problems for so long is a testament to their dedication and vision; that they finally succumbed to them is a shame, but no great surprise. Few of the supergroups who followed in Cream's wake lasted half as long for basically those reasons. It is worth emphasizing, though, that, good or bad, Cream cannot be held responsible for what came after.

Could Cream have achieved more or stayed together longer? Certain facts do militate against the idea; not least, the fiery history Jack and Ginger shared well before Cream, which blew up into the whole songwriting credit debate. Other problems, like the lack of a decent PA, could have been overcome, and all parties agree that if the management had let them alone and given them a long break much earlier, things might have been different. It's clear, though, that if Cream had gone on, things would have changed, and the three-piece jamming band would certainly have evolved into something else.

Since their demise, Cream has never been the subject of a fashionable cult, along the lines of The Doors or The Velvet Underground. Perhaps Cream's songs, while frequently sad or pessimistic, are simply not dark enough. Or perhaps sixteen-minute drum solos are intrinsically less hip than songs about Oedipal lust or shooting heroin. Nonetheless, Cream's albums have always been available and continue to sell in large quantities to new generations of rock fans. It's impossible to think of oldies radio stations not playing "Sunshine of Your Love" or "Tales of Brave Ulysses." That coupled with the recent revelation that George Harrison's son has the cover of *Disraeli Gears* stencilled on the back of his leather jacket says more about Cream's legacy than any amount of critical speculation.

CODA

Cream's final shows at The Royal Albert Hall, in November 1968, are not quite the end of the story. On January 12, 1993, Cream was inducted into the Rock and Roll Hall of Fame. Much to everybody's surprise, all three members not only turned up at the induction dinner in L.A., but played as well. On that night they played three numbers: "Sunshine of Your Love," "Crossroads," and, for the first time ever live, "Born Under a Bad Sign" (Jack never found the time, back in 1968, to master the simultaneous bass and vocal parts on the song). It was a competent performance, even if it inevitably lacked a little of their original spark, and the audience was left with the feeling that Cream *could* put something new together that wouldn't embarrass the band or their fans.

It was an emotional event for all three, with Clapton visibly weeping during his acceptance speech. About their playing together that night, Eric says, "It was just as if time had not taken its toll. We just played as if we were ready to do another tour, and it was the first day of rehearsal. We did 'Born Under a Bad Sign,' and we immediately adopted our old roles—the way we talked to one another, the humor came back , , it was just as if nothing had ever happened. And it was an extraordinarily uplifting experience, [a] very spiritual experience for me."

Eric goes on to describe his reaction, musically, to the other two, in what must be regarded as a very telling comment: "It's been so long since I've been around something from somebody else that inspires me like that. Because for the last twenty years, it's been up to me to inspire me."

The effect on Jack was just as profound. He says, "[The evening] was very long [and] by the time we got onstage to play, I think we were all

131

a bit emotionally drained. But if you're in a band, that's the amazing thing: there's a strength that exists beyond the individual members. There's something else that gives you the ability to do almost impossible things."

After the event, there was much speculation about a possible Cream reunion and, indeed, the three musicians seriously discussed the idea. The agreement between them was that, if it could been done properly, then they were all up for it. It's to their credit that none of them wanted to do a huge tour just for the money.

At the time of this writing, a reunion remains a theoretical possibility, but as the years pass, it seems more unlikely. Jack and Ginger have played together, along with guitarist Gary Moore, in a sub-Cream power trio, but perhaps Ginger is the most realistic when it comes to the real thing: "I really somehow doubt it will happen. In a way it's a shame, but I don't know. We made a statement when we were younger. That's it, that's enough. It's something to feel good about. I'd love to play with them again, I really would. But how, or when, or whether, or ever, who knows?"

APPENDIX

Richard Meltzer, a well-known rock critic noted as the writer of the most esoteric and obscure rock journalism of the era, wrote this unique review of *Disraeli Gears* for *Crawdaddy.*

What a Goddam Great Second Cream Album
>Mere uniqueness.[1]
>
>Cute little vocals on one end, and top-flight instrumental extravaganzas on the other, slammed together through some sort of Donovan-Zappa Avoidance Principle, too, just a little elusive to put the finger on.[2]
>
>Not an ounce of eschatological viscera.[3]
>
>With Cream, got to start with the NON-BUMMER GRID OF ANALYSIS: there are no true primary bummers, just non-bummers and non-non-bummers.
>
>Ginger drumming like crossing very early Ringo with football marching band, and that's no bummer altogether.[4] Ginger Baker is basi-

---

1. And, cause it's English, part of the English programmatic uniqueness scene, a stopover on the English Programmatic Uniqueness Trail and nothing could be finer.

2. So you have either unobvious Smiley Beach Boys and first-album Buckley or you have Bee Gees when they sound like soggy shredded wheat, which is sure okay.

3. But typewriters don't have any either, and typewriters are fine.

4. And man, look, there's the DRUMMER BUMMER: really listen to Ringo's "What Goes On" and then listen to Ginger's "Blue Condition," and who knows what will bubble through? Anyway, you got this drummer boy in each, accompanying his own mere vocal, and why bother saying it's not a bummer just 'cause it's a standard non-bummer guy with lots of apparant *ad hominem* pressure? 'Cause you wanna deal with it as *good?* Man, that's a drag. Why ignore the GRAND BUMMER just 'cause either bummers don't seem like moves anymore, or they're too much of a move and you don't wanna do the old Aristotelian piss-on-Plato move? 'Cept now you can deal with the NON-NON-BUMMER. Man, you can be sure the innovative and non-misunderstanding bummer move is approaching fast, but regretably not as fast as moves are getting played out. And someday soon Eric Burdon may accept the reemergence of Bobby Vee.

cally *pre*-Ringo, if you can imagine both of them in the archaeological scene.[5]

SWLABR, lots of Trini Lopez vocals by Jack Bruce. Sums up all that is or could be post-Balin. He accomplishes for a male vocalist, in "We're Going Wrong," what anything by Janis Joplin would do for a female, or something in that direction anyway.[6]

Only Duane Eddy or Bo Diddley could do a Dizzy Gillespie on guitar and Eric Clapton is—let's see, he's not either A or B, he's C: Clapton. So he *can't* be doin' the Diz. But he is doin—.

Waste is rest, and it's restful, not embarrassing, here, and it implies lack of education to the waste-labelers, a gimmick borrowed from jazz.

"Mother's Lament" suggests the Phil Spector studio intrusion on one of the early Righteous Brothers albums even more than it suggests "Naked If I Want To," or any other bell-ringers of that ilk.[7] Once upon a time, while it was playing, Memphis Sam donated the comment: "'Strange Brew' is nice."

Cream goes for words about seven years old and 4.2 months ahead of time, implicating themselves in simaltaneous necrophelia and prenatalophelia more obviously than do most with this combination as a necessity. "Got this thing, got to keep it sharp"[8] reminiscent of "Gettin' yer fork in the meat"[9] Words either folkie or Fuggy, so narrowly miss the NON-NON-NON-NON-NON-BUMMER RAP.

"Dance the Night Away" comes on like "Two Faces Have I" when that was fashionable and McGuinn when he was fashionable[10] plus an open window with snow mussin' around out there. No, it doesn't.

But this is mystery-book puberty, not physiological puberty, and one of those prostate massages advertized in the *LA Free Press* would likely do a lot of harm to Cream.[11]

---

5. In the archaeology cosmic framework, there is a basic BUMMER NEUTRALITY. So you can say all sorts of value-laden stuff about it, like it's good or bad, but with Cream here it doesn't matter before the fact rather than the other way, the way the Kinks pull it off.

0. Ask yourself tonight: What is vocal summation?

7. Whadda we do with all this "suggests" and "sounds like" stuff? Get it? Even when BUMMER OBSCURITY snaps out history as inadvertant unavoidable reference to obscurity has become tiresome even though it has.

8. In "Take it Back."

9. You useta hear it everywhere.

10. Nice manifestation of the fact that The Byrds played out the whole Byrds thing on their own, destroying an entire prior eternity which can only return as a NON-NON-NON-NON-BUMMER MOVE.

11. Although NSU will for all time signify the bike, here there's a hint of non-specific urethritis.

Thus I highly recommend *Disraeli Gears* (Atco 33–232).[12] Even more highly than the Strawberry Alarm Clock.

But hold on if you have to. That sure isn't enough data to make anybody go out into the cold to buy the album.[13] So here's more, okay? Sure.

Not even mere uniqueness, that is not even unique.

"Outside Woman Blues" is the[14]

"Sunshine of Your Love," right down to Clapton's "Blue Moon" reference pumice-like guitar plunkin', is hard-core RUBBER BAND MUSIC.[15]

"This tree is ugly and it wants to die" is part of the visual-literary bulk of the cover Zappa designed for *Absolutely Free*. He kept it visual-literary 'cause trees might just eat it as far as he was concerned or at least the concept of an ugly tree hit him only aesthetically or maybe it was all part of the non specific Polack joke new-content generation thing.[16] Cream's "World of Pain" is not only tree-pitying, but it is *musical* as well.[17]

"Tales of Brave Ulysses" is the remaining unmentioned track.

RICHARD MELTZER

---

12. All in all, the best and possibly less than the best record to play in the distance while your smoking it up in the bathroom and you walk out and everybody figures you took a shit or masturbated or something 'cause you look so long. Cream takes its time, too.

13. And what the fuck is the function of the art crtic if not precisely to get people to buy records?

14. Very finest oo-hoo, just the very best.

15. If you have a cold, go on: call it the RUBBER BUBBER, go ahead.

16. Well, at the very least he didn't mind exposing to ridicule and laughter the poor, wretched, death-oriented, repulsive TREE.

17. Well, maybe Zappa didn't wanna *sing* about it, maybe he really felt bad for the tree and ya know he jus' was bitterly satirizin' tree-hate and insensitivity to tree-sufferin' and yeah, that's it, he just couldn't get it up to sing about the whole morbid business. Let's hope that's it and listen to Cream anyway.

18. One of my favorite albums, the other being . . .

DISCOGRAPHY

Wrapping Paper / Cat's Squirrel

Reaction 591007 (released October 1966; No. 34)

I Feel Free / NSU

Reaction 591011 (released December 1966; No. 11)

Strange Brew / Tales of Brave Ulysses

Reaction 591015 (released June 1967; No. 17)

Anyone for Tennis / Pressed Rat and Warthog

Polydor 56 258 (released May 1968; No. 40)

Sunshine of Your love / SWLABR

Polydor 56 286 (released September 1968; No. 25)

White Room / Those Were the Days

Polydor 56 300 (released January 1969; No. 28)

Badge / What a Bringdown

Polydor 56 315 (released April 1969; No. 18)

I Feel Free / NSU
Atco 6462 (released January 1967)

Strange Brew / Tales of Brave Ulysses
Atco 6488 (released June 1967)

Spoonful / Spoonful Part 2
Atco 6522 (released c. September 1967)

Sunshine of Your Love / SWLABR
Atco 6544 (released February 1968; No. 5)

Anyone for Tennis / Pressed Rat and Warthog
Atco 6575 (released May 1968)

White Room / Those Were the Days
Atco 6617 (released October 1968; No. 6)

Crossroads / Passing the Time
Atco 6646 (released February 1969; No. 28)

Badge / What a Bringdown
Atco 6668 (released April 1969)

Sweet Wine / Hey Lawdy Mama
Atco 6708 (released c. August 1969)

Fresh Cream

Reaction 593001 (m) 594001 (s) (released December 1966, No. 6)
Side 1: *NSU / Sleepy Time Time / Dreaming / Sweet Wine / Spoonful*
Side 2: *Cat's Squirrel / Four Until Late / Rollin' and Tumblin' / I'm So Glad
/ Toad*

Disraeli Gears

Reaction 593003 (m) 593004 (s) (released November 1967, No. 5)
Side 1: *Strange Brew / Sunshine of Your Love / World of Pain / Dance the Night Away / Blue Condition / Tales of Brave Ulysses*
Side 2: *SWLABR / We're Going Wrong / Outside Woman Blues / Take It Back / Mother's Lament*

Wheels of Fire (Double LP)

Polydor 582 031/2 (m) 582 031/3 (s) (released August 1968, No. 3)
Part One: In the Studio
Side 1: *White Room / Sitting on Top of the World / Passing the Time / As You Said / Pressed Rat and Warthog*
Side 2: *Politician / Those Were the Days / Born under a Bad Sign / Deserted Cities of the Heart*
Part Two: Live at the Fillmore
Side 1: *Crossroads (Winterland 3/10/68, 1st set) / Spoonful (Winterland 3/10/68, 1st set)*
Side 2: *Traintime (Winterland 3/8/68, 1st set) / Toad (Fillmore Auditorium 3/7/68, 2nd set)*

Wheels of Fire: In the Studio (Single LP)

Polydor 582 033 (m)/ 583 033 (s) (released August 1968, No. 7)
Same tracks as double LP.

Wheels of Fire: Live at the Fillmore (Single LP)

Polydor 582 040 (m)/ 583 040 (s) (released August 1968)
Same tracks as double LP.

Goodbye

Polydor 583 053 (released March 1969, No. 1)
Side 1: *I'm So Glad (The Forum, Los Angeles, 10/19/68) / Politician (The Forum, Los Angeles, 10/19/68) / Sitting on Top of the World (The Forum, Los Angeles, 10/19/68)*
Side 2: *Badge / Doing That Scrapyard Thing / What a Bringdown*

Live Cream

Polydor 2383 016 (released June 1970, No. 4)
Side 1: *NSU (Winterland 3/10/68, 2nd set) / Sleepy Time Time (Winterland 3/9/68, 1st set)*
Side 2: *Sweet Wine (Winterland 3/10/68, 1st set) / Rollin' and Tumblin' (Fillmore Auditorium, 1st set) / Hey Lawdy Mama (studio 4/67)*

Live Cream Volume 2

Polydor 2383 119 (released June 1972, No. 15)
Side 1: *Deserted Cities of the Heart* (Oakland Coliseum, 10/4/68, 1st set)
      White Room (Oakland Coliseum, 10/4/68, 1st set)
      Politician (Oakland Coliseum, 10/4/68, 1st set)
      Tales of Brave Ulysses (Winterland, 3/10/68, 1st set)
Side 2: *Sunshine of Your Love* (Winterland, 3/9/68, 1st set)
      Steppin' Out (Winterland, 3/10/68, 1st set)

U.S. Albums

Cream's U.S. albums had the same track listings and release dates as the U.K. versions except *Fresh Cream,* which deleted "Spoonful" and added "I Feel Free" and was not released until March 1967. *Wheels of Fire* was released in June 1968 in the States, two months earlier than in England. Unlike in the U.K., it was never released as two separate albums.

The Atco catalog numbers and U.S. chart positions are as follows:

Fresh Cream	33–206 (m)/SD-33–206 (s)	No. 39
Disraeli Gears	33–232 (m)/SD-33–232 (s)	No. 4
Wheels of Fire	2–700 (m)/SD-2–700 (s)	No. 1
Goodbye	SD-7001	No. 2
Live Cream	SD-33–328	No. 15
Live Cream Vol. 2	SD-7005	No. 27

A rough mix of "Sunshine of Your Love," recorded at the Fillmore Auditorium on March 7, 1968, first set, was issued as a bonus track on Clapton's "After Midnight" CD single in 1988 (Polydor PZCD 8). It is otherwise unreleased.

When *Fresh Cream* was reissued in the U.K. in December 1974 (Polydor 284 067), three tracks were added: "I Feel Free," "Wrapping Paper," and "The Coffee Song." The latter had previously only been released in mainland Europe and had been unavailable for several years. This track listing has become the standard for all subsequent issues of the album throughout the world.

At the time of this writing, the best available issue of *Fresh Cream* is the DCC Gold Disc (GZS 1022). Not only is the remastering excellent, but in the course of researching tapes for the project, they discovered that "I'm So Glad" had only been recorded in mono. This means that most stereo versions of the album have fake stereo on "I'm So Glad." It's a pity, however, that DCC didn't use all the mono masters on the CD, since the stereo mix of *Fresh Cream* was vastly inferior to the mono one.

The Ultradisc/Mobile Fidelity Sound Lab version of *Disraeli Gears* (UDCD 562) uses complete sets of both the mono and stereo mixes, making it the most desirable issue of that album. However, despite claims to the contrary, there is no vast difference between the two mixes (certainly not as great as with *Fresh Cream*), and while the mono version may have a little more punch, many of the production effects can only be heard in stereo.

To date, the best digitally enhanced sound on a Cream album is on DCC's gold disk reissue of the complete *Wheels of Fire* (GSZ[2]1020)— the difference between their sound and that of the standard CD reissue is extraordinary. This version also features "Anyone for Tennis" (which also appears on the regular Polygram CD of *Goodbye*) plus an unedited "Passing the Time," which features approximately ninety seconds of the instrumental section sliced from the original release.

21 OCTOBER 1966	*Bandbeat:* Spoonful / Sleepy Time Time / Rollin' and Tumblin' (broadcast 21 November 1966)
8 NOVEMBER 1966	*Saturday Club:* Sweet Wine* / Steppin' Out* / Wrapping Paper* / Rollin' and Tumblin' / I'm So Glad / Sleepy Time Time (broadcast 12 November 1966)
21 NOVEMBER 1966	*Monday, Monday:* playlist unknown (broadcast live)

28 November 1966	*Guitar Club:* Crossroads / Sitting on Top of the World / Steppin' Out (broadcast 30 December 1966)
9 December 1966	*R&B Show:* Cat's Squirrel* / Traintime* / Hey Lawdy Mama* / I'm So Glad* (broadcast 9 January 1967)
10 January 1967	*Saturday Club:* Four until Late* / I Feel Free* / Traintime* / NSU* / Toad (broadcast 14 January 1967)
16 January 1967	*Monday, Monday:* playlist unknown (broadcast live)
25 January 1967	*Parade of the Pops:* playlist unknown (broadcast live)
27 March 1967	*Monday, Monday:* playlist unknown (broadcast live)
30 May 1967	*Saturday Club:* Strange Brew* / Tales of Brave Ulysses* / We're Going Wrong* (broadcast 3 June 1967)
4 July 1967	*Joe Loss Show:* playlist unknown (broadcast live)
24 October 1967	*Top Gear:* Take It Back* / Outside Woman Blues* / Tales of Brave Ulysses / Sunshine of Your Love / Born under a Bad Sign* (broadcast 29 October 1967)
9 January 1968	*Top Gear:* SWLABR* / Politician / Steppin' Out* / We're Going Wrong* / Blue Condition (broadcast 14 January 1968)

Only those tracks marked with an asterisk are known to exist in the BBC archives. Most exist because shortly after their original broadcasts, they were used as part of a long-running radio show called "Top of the Pops." This weekly show was compiled from recent sessions by a variety of acts, transferred to transcription disk, and sold to radio stations around the world. It was hosted by Brian Matthew (who was also the compere of

"Saturday Club"), which is why he introduces many of the songs, rather than the original DJs, like John Peel.

The only session that exists in its original tape form is the one recorded on September 12, 1966, for the BBC World Service R & B Show. This exists because the presenter, Alexis Korner, saved the tape. It is very possible that he also saved the complete October 1967 Top Gear session, because he rebroadcast it on the R & B Show. It's also possible that other presenters, producers, or engineers could have saved any of the sessions, but this cannot be confirmed. It is highly unlikely, however, that any of the live (i.e., not prerecorded) shows exist, unless they were recorded by enthusiasts off-air. While plenty of people seem to have recorded the Saturday Clubs and the Top Gears, no home tapes of any of the "missing" shows have ever surfaced.

The above list is believed to be complete, as the BBC archives have been thoroughly researched by Ken Garner (see "Works Consulted" in the Bibliography), but he admits that the files on a number of '60s shows are missing. Several Cream tape collectors list a session from Easy Beat (a genuine BBC show of the period) broadcast in May 1967 that features "Take It Back" and "Tales of Brave Ulysses." This is entirely possible, but cannot be confirmed.

To date only two Cream BBC tracks have been officially released—"Hey Lawdy Mama," from Alexis Korner's R & B Show and the January 1968 Top Gear version of "Steppin' Out." Both are on the 1988 Clapton box set Crossroads (Polydor 422 835261–2). If the various interested parties can reach an agreement, however, more BBC Cream material is likely to appear.

An objective evaluation of the BBC tracks is difficult. Certainly they are of historical interest, since, if nothing else, they form a considerable alternative body of work. They also bridge the gap between studio and live recordings, as they were invariably recorded on first take, with no overdubs. However, they lack the genuine spontaneity of live performance and audience response. Conversely, although all the sessions were competently recorded—and avoid the worst of Stigwood's production shortcomings—there were no Felix Pappalardis or Tom Dowds among the BBC staff. Consequently, most of the tracks sound rather stiff and formal, not to say naked.

Many bands who did sessions for the BBC took the opportunity to play material they did not normally perform or record. Unfortunately, of the extant Cream tracks, there are none that they did not release in one form or another elsewhere. Likewise, the arrangements are, by Cream's standards, very simple, the one exception being "I'm So Glad," which includes Clapton's musical quote from the "1812 Overture," something he did regularly early on, but abandoned before the number was (officially) recorded live. Nonetheless, despite the reservations, the legitimate release of Cream's BBC sessions is something most of their fans would thoroughly approve of, even though they probably have most of them already via re-broadcasts or on bootlegs.

Live Tapes

This list is restricted to *Disraeli Gears* period material, i.e., April–November 1967. It is, however, a complete list of all known tapes from that era.

22 APRIL 1967	*Ricky Tick, Hounslow, U.K.:* Sunshine of Your Love / Hey Lawdy Mama / Sweet Wine / Rollin' and Tumblin' / Spoonful (cut) / Toad
MAY 1967	*Empire Pool, Wembley, U.K.:* NSU (cut) / I'm So Glad
27 MAY 1967	*Tulip Bulb Auction Hall, Spalding, U.K.:* unknown
3 SEPTEMBER 1967	*Fillmore Auditorium, San Francisco, Calif.:* Spoonful / Tales of Brave Ulysses / Sunshine of Your Love / Sweet Wine / NSU / Hey Lawdy Mama / Sleepy Time Time / Steppin' Out (cut)
7 SEPTEMBER 1967	*Psychedelic Supermarket, Boston, Mass.:* Sunshine of Your Love / Spoonful / Tales of Brave Ulysses / Sweet Wine (cut)
9 SEPTEMBER 1967	*Brandeis University, Waltham, Mass.:* Tales of Brave Ulysses / Sunshine of Your Love / NSU / Sitting on Top of the World / Steppin' Out / Traintime / Toad
15 OCTOBER 1967	*Grande Ballroom, Detroit, Mich.:* Tales of Brave Ulysses / NSU / Sitting on Top of the World /

Sweet Wine / Rollin' and Tumblin' / Spoonful /
Steppin' Out / Traintime / Toad / I'm So Glad

14 NOVEMBER 1967   *Konserthus, Stockholm, Sweden:* Tales of Brave
Ulysses / Sunshine of Your Love / Sleepy Time
Time / Steppin' Out / Traintime / Toad (cut) / I'm
So Glad

Unfortunately, most of the above tapes are poor sound quality audience recordings. Nonetheless, they are of great historical interest, especially the Fillmore tape. One or two of them, however, are of better sound quality. The Ricky Tick tape *is* an audience recording, but a superior one. It was recorded by a blues enthusiast and sometime independent record label owner, the late Ian Sippen. He knew Cream, and they apparently gave him permission to record, which he did, using a reel-to-reel machine, with two mikes set up in front of the stage. Although the results are not perfect, the tape really captures the atmosphere of the gig, which took place at a vital time in the band's evolution—between the two sets of *Disraeli Gears* recording sessions. There is a remarkable clarity to the instruments and vocals, and the recording is not swamped by crowd noise—the norm for most audience tapes of this era. This tape has been issued as a bootleg CD as *Ricky Tick Live* (Scorpio 93066). The disk also contains three tracks from the November 15, 1966, Klook's Kleek gig and some Clapton-era Yardbirds material.

Sippen also recorded the May 27 Spalding show. However, at the time of this writing, the tape is still in the hands of its current owner, so no comments as to the sound quality or the performance can be made here.

The Grande tape was much touted by collectors when it first surfaced because of its supposedly unbeatable sound quality. While it's true that it certainly isn't an audience recording (most likely it was made off of the Grande's soundboard), and the tape that first entered circulation is obviously close to the master, the mix is terrible, with the bass all but inaudible. This is a great shame, because although the playing isn't as exotic as on the Fillmore tape from September (no raga sounds on "Spoonful," for example), it's the most complete recording of the band on the first U.S. tour and is probably culled from more than one set.

The Grande show has been bootlegged more than once, the best version being *Real Cream* (Gold Standard RC 01/2). This double CD also features four of the unreleased rough mixes from the Winterland March 1968 show. The most recent issue of the tape (*Cream Set*) features similar sound quality, but the bonus material—from Texas on the Farewell tour—isn't as good as its counterpart on *Real Cream*.

The Swedish shows are not audience tapes either, and may well have been a radio broadcast recorded off air. Unfortunately, it seems that that the fan who taped the March show did a better job than the one who taped the later performance, as the sound on the November tape is somewhat muffled. As with the BBC tapes it is possible that master recordings exist somewhere. A release of both of those shows in perfect quality might just produce the best possible live Cream recordings.

BIBLIOGRAPHY

Books

Coleman, R. *Survivor.* London, 1985.

Cunningham, M. *Good Vibrations: A History of Record Production.* London, 1996.

Kooper, A. *Backstage Passes.* New York, 1972.

Neville, R. *Hippie Hippie Shake.* London, 1995.

Roberty, M. *Eric Clapton: The Complete Recording Sessions 1963–1992.* London, 1993.

Sandford, C. *Clapton: Edge of Darkness.* London, 1994.

Turner, S. *Conversations with Clapton.* London, 1976.

Periodicals

"A Frenzy of Whipped Cream in New York." *Melody Maker,* 22 April 1967.

"At Last The Cream Do Themselves Justice." *Melody Maker,* 11 August 1968.

"Cream Declare War on Singles." *Melody Maker,* 18 November 1967.

"Cream: *Disreali Gears.*" *Beat Instrumental,* ca. November 1968.

Delehant, J. "An Interview with Eric Clapton." *Hit Parader.*

———. "Cream: *Disreali Gears.*" *Billboard,* ca. November 1968.

Edmonds, B. "Motor City's Burning." *Off the Wall,* no. 5 (1993): 4.

"Felix Pappalardi: Solving Modern Studio Problems." *Hit Parader,* March 1968, 40–41.

Goldstein, R. "Cream: They Play Blues Not Superstar." *Village Voice,* 10 May 1967, 20, 21, 25.

Hall, C. "Cream: Group That's Cream of Rock Crop." *Billboard,* October 1967.

"Hendrix: Blind Date." *Melody Maker,* 10 June 1967.

Jones, N. "Cream: It's Just a Fact That We're Heavy Musicians." *Rolling Stone,* 24 February 1968.

Landau, J. "Goody Guys and Bad Guys." *Eye,* October 1968.

Logan, N. "Jack Bruce on *Goodbye.*" *Hit Parader,* ca. April 1969.

Pappalardi, F. "How Cream Made *Wheels of Fire.*" *Hit Parader,* February 1969, 12–15.

"The Creation of Pure Energy from the Cream." *Melody Maker,* 11 October 1967.

Tobler, J., and P. Frame. "Jack Bruce's Musical Tree." *Zigzag,* no. 22 (1971): 4–6, 22.

Van Lustbader, E. "Climbing from Cream to Mountain: Felix Pappalardi." *Circus* ca. 1971.

Wenner, J. "Cream: *Disraeli Gears.*" *Rolling Stone,* 20 January 1968.

Wickham, V. "Mountain . . . Involved." *Hit Parader,* September 1967, 28–35.

Williams, P. "Interviewed: Felix Pappalardi." *Crawdaddy,* ca. 1968.

Works Consulted

Books

Eric, Jack and Ginger: The Cream Complete. London: Wise Publications, 1972.

Garner, K. *In Session Tonight: The Complete Radion One Recordings.* London, 1993.

Hogg, B., and B. Whitaker. *Cream in Gear.* London, 1991.

Picardi, J., and D. Wade. *Atlantic and the Godfathers of Rock & Roll.* London, 1993.

Platt, J. *London's Rock Routes.* London, 1985.

Platt, J., C. Dreja, and J. McCarty. *Yardbirds.* London, 1984.

Roberty, M. *The Eric Clapton Scrapbook.* London, 1994.

Shapiro, H. *Graham Bond: The Mighty Shadow.* London, 1992.

———. *Slowhand: The Story of Eric Clapton.* London, 1984.

Tobler, J., and S. Grundy. *The Record Producers.* London, 1982.

Periodicals

Dowd, T. "The Emergence of the Multitrack Era." *EQ,* October 1993, 69–78.

Also consulted were *Disc & Music Echo,* various issues, 1966–1968; *Melody Maker,* various issues, 1966–1968; and the *Record Mirror,* various issues, 1966–1968.

INDEX

149

Clapton, Eric (*cont.*)
    on San Francisco scene, 96–97, 99
    on singles *vs.* albums, 113
    on "Sunshine" composition date, 75
    on *What's Shakin'* compilation, 22
    opinion of Disraeli Gears, 86
    possible performance with Blues Incorporated, 8
    Sharp and, 43
    singing of, 82
    Tiny Tim and, 96
    use of wah-wah pedal, 77, 81
    with Yardbirds, 10, 12–14, 19
"Clearout, The," 57, 58
Coasters, The, 64
"Coffee Song, The," 28, 141
Coleman, Ray, *Survivor,* 20–21
Collins, Gail, 82, 84
    lyrics for "Strange Brew," 70–72
Collins, Judy, 78
Coltrane, John, 107
Colyer, Ken, 3
Condon, Eddie, 2
Conley, Arthur, 64
Cooper, Michael, 93
Crawdaddy (periodical)
    Pappalardi interview, 66
    review of *Disraeli Gears,* 133–35
Crawdaddy (Richmond club), 12
"Crawling Up a Hill," 15
Cream. *See also* Baker, Peter "Ginger"; Bruce, Jack; Clapton, Eric; *specific albums and songs*
    achievements and influence of, 128–30
    ads and posters for, *24, 25, 47, 89, 103, 104–105, 110, 111, 114, 118–19, 122–24*
    American tour of, 45–53
    BBC radio sessions, 68, 141–44
    blues covers of, 33–35
    breakup of, 75, 122–24, 130
    business affairs of, 24, 122
    composer attribution problems of, 33–36
    debut of, 24
    in Detroit, 106–107, 109
    dress of, 48

    early gigs of, 25–28
    East Coast tour, 104
    European bookings of, 44
    farewell tour, 125–26
    formation of, ix, 1, 19–22
    group dynamics of, 23–24, 33, 57, 96, 117, 123, 125, 129–30
    Hall of Fame induction, 131–32
    humor of, 81
    improvisations of, 101–102, 120–21, 128
    live tapes of, 38–39, 68, 76, 100, 118–21, 144–46
    London bookings of, 42–44
    London Polytechnic gig, 25–26
    in Los Angeles, 103
    Marshall stacks of, 59, *60,* 74
    miscellaneous tapes of, 115
    motion picture announced for, 45–46
    Murray the K gig, 46–53, 60
    musical styles of, 22–23, 41–42, 85–86, 101–102, 112–13, 115, 118
    in New York, 46–53, 104–106
    "no singles" policy of, 113
    Polytechnic gig, 37
    popularity of, 112, 130
    possible reunion of, 132
    psychedelic equipment of, 48
    Rayrik sessions, 28, 35
    reviews of, 24, 28, 89–90, 106, 109, 110–12, 121, 133–35
    Roundhouse gig, 42
    Ryemuse sessions, 35–37, 54–58
    in San Francisco, 97–103, 118–21
    in Scotland, 91–96
    set list of, 102, 116
    studio behavior of, 66
    studio *vs.* live styles, 100–102, 113, 118, 123–24, 129
    trio *vs.* quartet format of, 20–22
    virtuosity of, 28
    volume level of, 106, 121–22
Cream Set (bootleg album), 146
Crosby, David, 85
"Crossroad Blues," 34–35
"Crossroads," 22, 23
    attribution of, 34–35

Lovin' Spoonful, The, 21
"Lulu Show" (BBC show), 75

M

Madison Square Garden (New York),
    125–26
Mandala, 46
Manfred Mann, 17, 20, 21
Manny's (music store), 48, 77
Mardin, Arif, 62, 63, 64, 68
Marquee, The (London club), 8, 12, 29
"Married Woman Blues," 84
Marsh, Dave, Before I Get Old, 52
Martin, Charlotte, 43, 92
Martin, George, 37
Masters, Robert, 24, 42
Matthew, Brian, 142–43
Mayall, John, 14–16, 20
    differences with Clapton, 18
Mayfair Productions. See Ryemuse
    (Mayfair Productions)
MC5, 107, 109
McCarty, Jim, 13
McClure, Michael, 97
McGhee, Brownie, 39
McGuinness, Tom, 11
McHarg, Jim, 7
McLaughlin, John, 9, 44
McNair, Harold, 5
McVie, John, 15
"Meet Me in the Bottom," 38, 39
Melly, George, on Trad jazz, 4
Melody Maker (periodical), 1, 3, 62
    "Blind Date" reviews, 89–90
    Clapton interview, 49, 51, 57, 86,
        113
    Disraeli Gears review, 110
    review of Cream debut, 24
Meltzer, Richard, review of Disraeli Gears,
    133–35
Memphis Slim, 34
Metropolis Blues Quartet, 11–12
Middle Earth (London club), 42, 43, 96
Miles, Buddy, 53
Miller, Steve, 93
Mississippi Sheiks, 115
modal music, 100–101
Modern Jazz Quartet, 64–65
"Monday Monday" (BBC show), 141–42
Monkees, The, 85

Monterey Pop Festival, 96–97
Moon, Keith, 51
Moore, Gary, 132
Moscoso, Victor, 93
"Mother's Lament," 81, 88, 113
    discography of, 139
    reviews of, 134
Mouse, Stanley, 93
Move, The, 86
Murray the "K" (Murray Kaufman), 46–53,
    60

N

National Jazz and Blues Federation
    Festival, 10, 24
Neil, Fred, 66
NEMS, 45, 47
Neville, Richard, 78
    Hippie Hippie Shake, 43
New Departures (jazz/poetry series), 29,
    43
New Musical Express (periodical), poll
    winners concert, 73
"Ninety-Nine Blues," 84
"NSU," 23, 37, 102
    BBC radio sessions, 142
    discography of, 138
    improvising on, 100
    live tapes of, 38, 39, 121, 140,
        144

O

Ochs, Phil, 46
Off the Wall (periodical), 109
Oliver, Joseph "King," 3
Oliver, Paul, 34
"On Top of the World," 15
100, The (London club), 12
Ory, Kid, 2
"Outside Woman Blues," 23, 115
    BBC radio sessions, 142
    composer credit on, 34
    discography of, 139
    reviews of, 112, 135
    session work on, 84
Oz (periodical), 43

P

Palmer, Ben, 11
    on Atlantic sessions, 63

ABOUT THE AUTHOR

John A.Platt is a well-known authority on Sixties rock and culture. He is the author of several books, including *The Yardbirds, London's Rock Routes* and *Inside the Experience,* a biography of Jimi Hendrix. He has worked as a consultant on numerous television and video documentaries, including Polygram's definitive *Fresh Live Cream* (for which he conducted the interviews and wrote the script) and the VH1 *Legends* series, notably the one on Eric Clapton, which he also narrated. He also produces archive albums for reissue and has curated seasons of rock films at the National Film Theatre in London and Lincoln Center in New York. A teenager during the heady days of mid-Sixties London, he recently migrated to New York's Greenwich Village, where he lives with his American wife.